# POWER PR

## A Streetfighter's
## Handbook To
## Winning Public Relations

# POWER PR

## A Streetfighter's Handbook To Winning Public Relations

### BY DENNIS COLE HILL

**FELL PUBLISHERS, INC.**

Hollywood, Florida

Library of Congress Cataloging-In-Publication Data

Hill, Dennis Cole.
 Power PR / Dennis Cole Hill.
  p.    cm.

 ISBN 0-8119-0650-7  :  $14.95
 1. Public relations.  I. Title.
HD59.H48   1990
629.2--dc20                                                          90-3109
                                                                        CIP


Library of Congress Catalog Card Number  90-3109
International Standard Book Number:    0-8119-0650-7

For information address:
    Fell Publishers, Inc.
    2131 Hollywood Boulevard
    Hollywood, Florida 33020


Manufactured in the United States of America
1234567890

# Dedication

To my mother who makes all dreams possible; and to my dear wife, who makes them happen.

# Acknowledgments

I would like to especially thank my brother, Dean, and his wife, Nancy, for all their first rate editing skills, and the rest of my family for their patience and support; the Financial Resources Group for their help with the cover; Allan and Joe at Fell, for all their work; David Bradley, photographer; and, of course, Sandy.

A very special thanks to Ray Kennedy and Paul Zindell, without whose training, patience, concern, inspiration and friendship through the years, this project would never have been attempted.

DCH

# Contents

# POWER PR
## More Than
## Free Advertising

Ever wonder why somebody's name with such-and-such company seems to always be in the newspaper? Or why one of your competitors gets interviewed on the evening news? Ever wonder why people who go to buy a certain product automatically think of Joe's store up the street — instead of yours?

It's not because they have better products, necessarily. Not because they're better looking. No. They are sharp business persons who recognize the value of public relations and go for it. Simple. As simple as this book.

Many of the world's largest companies are changing the way they think about marketing. Gone are the days when they simply bought ads and sold their products. More and more companies are allocating much percentages of their marketing dollars to public relations and promotions. Why? These companies have found that a strong PR and promotions program is more effective in so many more

1

and different ways than advertising alone. Simply — they make more money. You can, too.

Put the **Power** in your corner! Right now, you can have your business, company, restaurant, franchise, professional practice, or community service organization up and running with a full-fledged public relations and promotional program that will make as much money for you as you would make hiring a Pro! And, best of all, it won't cost you much more than your time.

If you can grasp the basic concepts of what public relations is and how it can affect the speedy growth of your business, firm, or practice, the power is in your hand. This book will give you the proven step-by-step guidance and instruction.

The practice of primary public relations is very simple:

> **It is a supplementary communications and marketing link to your customers, future customers, and your community.**

Two key points to remember:

1) **Nothing is exact.**

2) **Everything is flexible.**

Just because you take the time and energy to design a program doesn't mean it can't be altered or improved upon to fit any individual circumstance. Your own good judgement provides the basic criteria on which you should base any public relations activity or decision.

In theory, everyone in business is always performing is some sort of public relations: playing on the company softball team, answering phones during a local fund drive, coaching a little league team, joining networking associations, winning awards, just meeting people at a party. Even so, many of these types of activities go unnoticed because nobody takes the time to let people know — primarily through the media. So much of what we do in life is important, and it may even be interesting to others. Yet, because we're either shy, humble, or whatever, no one notices.

Public relations is more than just free advertising. It lends credibility to your company, keeping you a step ahead of the competition. In this respect, it is a supplementary sales tool, one on which you can build. You create a positive image of community goodwill and trust which will follow you and your employees every where you go.

One of the key accomplishments of a good overall PR program is the creation of an identity for your company. (See Chapter Five for more on identity.) For what and in what light do you want your company to be known?

From the time we are children, most of us are taught to be humble: "Don't be a show-off. Tone down the old ego." This is good advice, and we shouldn't be spouting off every time we do something we think is great. But look at it this way: By letting people know we're involved, that we care about ourselves and others in our communities, we might spur others on to accomplishing task in their work, their community, or their industry. As altruistic as it may sound, that's why you should start your **Power PR** program today.

Of course, big profits along the way won't hurt, either.

# CHAPTER ONE

# GETTING STARTED
## Your Plan
## For Success

Your PR program is like your business plan — you simply set your goals and map your route to achieving them. But first, we must teach you to:

## THINK NEWS!

To get your PR program moving in the right direction, start looking at your business in a new light. Begin developing a "nose for news." Even though you know your company better than anyone else, look around your office, your plant, your store. Notice what's going on — the *who*, *what*, *where*, *why*, *when*, and *how* of your entire operation.

Seriously examine the equipment and the surroundings. What makes your business unique? Why in heaven's name do you have an advantage over the competition? What, specifically, makes you different and better than the other guy? Open your eyes: Is your plant manager a boxer, a tournament chess player? Does your secretary coach a

Pop Warner football team? Have any of your sales people recently completed a training course? Have they broken any sales records? Any new faces around? Any new equipment? How will it help your clients? What's happening in your industry, and what's your role in that change/growth/decline? How have you been adapting? In short, what makes your business tick, and why is it so exciting that you're in it in the first place? Discovering who you are and what you have is the essential basis of a powerful PR program. It's actually quite simple — notice things.

Now read the paper. And, I mean **read** the whole paper, not just the Business, Sports and Editorial sections. Read it cover to cover and notice what is on the front pages, and what's in the City, Fashion, Real Estate, Entertainment, Lifestyle, Gardening, Home Improvement, and TV sections. The amount of news generated by PR people may surprise you.

On the front page, most of the national news stories require the involvement of the PR departments of the various government agencies. When you read a statement from a congressman, you can almost be sure his PR person called the media to hear it (or sent out a statement).

Other than the usual fires, murders and car accidents (handled by the police or fire department PR person), the stories in your city section are filled with quotes from the mayor, school district director, and local notables given to the press by PR people.

PR people arranged most of the interviews, supplied all the player photos, and provided nearly all of the capsulized player histories and statistics in the sports section.

Virtually all of the entertainment section is supplied by PR people eager to have their stars' faces grab your attention. The fashion section is generally the product of clothes designers, manufacturers and retailers.

"Acme Company Sets Record Profit" headlines the business section, and it came from the corporate PR office. The interviews for the story were also arranged through the PR office.

If you've ever read the phrase, "A spokesman for so-and-so said..." you can count on the spokesman being a PR person. As you can see, nearly all of what you read in the paper somehow involves a PR person somewhere along the line.

TV is not that much different, except that it relies more heavily on the visual. (Press conferences are usually held for TV.) TV news requires that people who have something to say do so in front of the camera. (If Dan Rather's entire newscast was nothing more than him repeating what other people said, it would be as exciting as watching grass grow.)

So, what has evolved is a cooperative relationship between the PR industry and the media. But no rule exists that says you can't be your own PR representative. You don't necessarily have to act like one, but begin to think like one.

## GETTING STARTED

Getting started is simple.

Begin with your general business plan. If your don't have one, make one. Just rough out where you want to be in three months, six months, a year, and five years. Be specific as you can and as creative as you like, but remember. If your general business plan covers five years, with review stops every three to six months, perhaps even every month with weekly progress analyses, your overall PR program should be of the same type and integrated with your general business plan.

You integrate your PR plan into your general business

plan by taking into consideration your goals — where you plan to be at what point in time.

**Example:**

You plan for your business to have grown fifteen percent in the next six months, you've hired a new sales person, and you're expecting a new product from a main supplier. Taking everything into consideration — money, time, and the significance of the situation — you'll tailor your PR efforts accordingly for that particular time period:

1. Two press releases and photos
    a. New sales person
    b. New product
2. An open house for the media/your clients
3. Follow-up calls
4. Luncheon at your store for product announcement

Flexibility is key, and you're not tied to any tightly regimented format. Allow yourself the freedom to change and adapt to fresh circumstances and new ideas as they occur. Suppose you have scheduled a news release on a new employee to be sent out this month. One of your suppliers introduces a revolutionary new product. Your release on your new employee should be put on a back burner in light of this more important news. By including the new product in the new employee release when it goes out a week or two later, you increase the value of the release by increasing the exposure of the new product.

Public Relations is not just *attracting attention*! It's attracting the right kind of attention as that attentions applies to any given situation. Naturally, if the new product is nothing great (you'll have to be the judge of this one), you won't want to do anything major. However, if the new product is something unique, especially if you're the only one in town who has it, then you do something special.

The point is that anyone can get attention by standing naked in the park. But stand in the park naked to protest teenage drug abuse, and you may bring some attention to bear on the important issue of drugs.

## STEP-BY-STEP

You'll need materials for this: a pad, pen or pencil, and an open mind. The keys: Begin now and *keep it simple!*

1. Examine your business plan, looking at what you foresee as some major upcoming events. Jot them down.

2. Look over those notes and think about where you want to be in terms of those events (be specific): working on twelve accounts by November; grossing over $50 a month in Widget sales by January; receiving four calls a day from prospective new clients two months from now; or increasing overall sales by fifteen percent by May.

   Now, think about your business, its people, their roles, their special talents as you see them. Think about your company, your industry and your market, and jot these ideas down, too.

3. Take each goal, and write out what it will take to get there in terms of a business decision. If you want to sell $50 a month in widgets by January, you can't sit around and wait for the market to find you. (People make markets; markets don't make people.)

We will enhance each decision with proven PR methods. For example:

   a.  Goal: to sell $50 in pencils in January.

   b.  Business decisions: Increase daily pencil sales calls on pencils by X percent, lower prices by X percent, offer bulk purchase specials, place one salesman in charge of widgets for January.

   c.  PR decisions: produce press releases: "John Smith Appointed Director of Pencil Sales At Acme," "Industry Predicts Increase in Pencil Demand," "Widget Industry Sees Price Cuts," etc.

It's simple. Just think of all the things that make pencils (or whatever) valuable. Again, examine your role in creating that value. You're the authority on pencils, and don't forget it!

Now, take all those specific goals you have assembled for your company, and do the exact same thing for each and every one of them.

Expanding your program is just as easy. Look at the following program, and see how it can be adapted to fit your needs. Note how this real program addresses the needs and goals of the company.

# ACME MARINE

## Overview

Acme Marine is a multi-level, complete marine facility. They service all boating and fishing needs for their immediate area. They offer sales and service of a variety of boats. They will soon offer the second of only tow marinas allowed by the state on the John's Reservoir, the state's largest and most populated water body.

Overall marketing efforts to this point have been essentially word of mouth, on-site signage, and various newspaper advertisements. The addition of the new marina will necessarily force an increase in the areas covered by marketing and PR to a statewide campaign.

Public relations efforts have been virtually none. However, the new marina has generated an abundancy of publicity. This publicity has created a fairly solid image of Acme Marine and the marina itself within the area. Nevertheless, many skeptics still exist.

The goal of our public relations plan is to enhance the awareness and the image of the marina throughout the state. It will also be our goal to sway the skeptics. Those who view the company as one of instability will quickly replace that image with one of safety, stability, and smooth operation. The marina will capitalize on an increased positive awareness, resulting in greater sales.

## Program and Plan

The primary goal of this PR program is to increase the awareness of ACME's new marina throughout the state on various levels. The boating public as well as the other dealers need to know about it. Also, it is necessary

## ACME
## MARINE
**Continued**

to get the word out to all skeptics that the marina is accomplishing everything it said it would accomplish.

Because the boating season is primarily the summer and construction on the new marina will be completed in early March, we target our grand opening for May. This will give us the balance of March and the month of April to make the necessary arrangements. Our plan consists of the following program and special events series:

1. Grand Opening:

    a.  A fishing tournament at the Reservoir, with the awards presentations at the Grand Opening Luncheon. (A special media personality category will be included.)

    b.  The Grand Opening Luncheon will include all appropriate local, state and federal personnel, possibly even the governor. The highest ranking and most recognizable official will cut the grand opening ribbon and award the tournament trophies and prizes. If possible, the luncheon will be held, under a tent in the marina parking lot. A speakers' table will include VIP's and marina principals, and short talks will be given by several attendees. Press throughout the state will be invited to attend.

    c.  A short press conference will be held following the luncheon, and boats will be

**ACME
MARINE**
**Continued**

available for on-the-water press tours of the
lake and marina. (Be sure to announce the
boat rides item in **all** news releases.)

d. A series of advance press releases with
photos and invitations will be mailed to
announce the opening, and follow-up
releases will re-confirm the event. Follow-up
calls will be made to all local media.

## 2. Ongoing Promotion

We will begin monthly announcements and "media
events" to continually increase the awareness of the
marina. We will design events that will attract both
boaters and the media throughout the season, perhaps
culminating in a festival of sorts at the end of the season.

*June*   Bass Month! Whoever catches the
largest bass in John's Reservoir will win a
new trolling motor and a depthfinder,
courtesy of Acme Marine. The challenge will
be issued statewide, with a special division
and prizes for the media.

*July*   "A Day At The Lake!" Acme Marine will
sponsor a day at the lake. We will offer boat
rides for $2 each around the lake, pull water
skiers for $15 a ride, and sponsor a picnic
with a band for the community. We will also
have an all-day fishing challenge for kids
twelve and under. All proceeds — above
and beyond expenses — will benefit the
local rehabilitation center for handicapped

## ACME MARINE

**Continued**

children. We will send out advance press releases to all local media, and contact the local newspaper for special inexpensive ad rates in exchange for a sponsorship. We will send out follow-up releases and photos detailing the amount raised.

*August*   Our new "Mach 21" boat line will be in by this time. This is a very special boat, and we are the only dealer in the state to carry it. We will send out releases to all media throughout the state. We will also invite the reporters on a fishing trip in the "Mach 21" anytime during the month. Also, while the weather is warm, we will make the "Mach 21" available to the fashion editor of the local paper for the annual swimsuit/summerwear photo spread.

*September*   We will begin providing the business reporters with an "annual" state of the industry report, detailing the activity of the boating industry throughout the state. We will examine the impact of the industry in this state, and we will get the national figures from the boating trade association in Washington, our primary motor manufacturer, and our main boat supplier.

*October*   As the boating season comes to a close, we will sponsor an "End of the Season Boat Show and Festival." We will invite the other local dealers to participate, and we will follow the same general pattern as the spring party. However, by adding the boat show on the lake, we will be able to clear out some of the remaining inventory.

*November*   Contact local travel agent and arrange winter fishing trip to warm climate for December. Get group rates, guides, etc. (Groups and tours get free accommodations for certain people — you and a reporter or two — if they have enough people.) In the dead of winter in a cold climate, many reporter/editors will jump at the chance for a free trip to seventy-five degrees, even if they'll have to do a little work. They'll not only cover your outing, but they'll have a travel item, a fishing technique story, a new equipment story, and a human interest story. Sell all this to a reporter in your invitation, and his editor will probably want to go instead.)

*December*   Fishing trip. Send photos and releases on big catches, attendees, etc., to local media. Organize Christmas boat parade. Encourage boaters from the local area to decorate their boats with lights, etc. Request local dignitaries (mayor, city council person, etc.) to be judges. Send advance releases to local media.

## ACME MARINE
**Continued**

*January*   We will announce our participation in the annual statewide boat show to all local media. We will also announce any new lines or products acquired and prepared for the show.

*February*   Make and distribute "Calendar of Events" for the next three/six months.

*March*   Begin organizing and promoting April Fishing tournament.

*April*   We will sponsor and organize the first fishing tournament of the season at the lake, and our marina will be the home base for all activities. Press releases will be sent to all statewide media; guides and boats will be provided for all reporters who wish to participate. Again, we will have a special media category for all participating reporters.

*May*   1st Anniversary Celebration.

This program is solid, simple, and inexpensive. Note that the dealership's expenses are minimal, and the program makes use of what the dealership has on hand — unsold trolling motors & depthfinders, the lake, boats, and fishing equipment. All that is added is the time it takes to organize everything. It may seem like a lot, but it's not. By dividing the responsibilities of each promotion among employees, each can plan to spend an hour or two a week on PR.

With this program, Acme's name will soon be connected with good events as they relate to their industry, community service, and quality products. They can expect to become known as good business people who recognize their role in the community. All of this leads to the most important aspect of the business: increased sales throughout the year.

## YOUR MEDIA LIST

Your media list is key to your program. You must get the right information to the right people in the press. You wouldn't send a tip on your top salesman winning a sales award to the fashion editor. News intended for the business section should go to the business section...fashion news goes to the fashion editor.

Assembling your list is easy. Just look through your local papers to find out who's in charge of what. Usually, editors also write some stories, and they are so listed in the section for which they write. Jot these down on Sunday mornings as you read your paper, and begin a master file. If you can't find the editor for a particular section, call the paper and ask who's in charge of what. Don't be shy. As I said, news people rely on their contacts for information, and you are a contact. The papers will be glad to give you whatever information you may need.

The same holds true for the TV and radio stations in town. In TV, you can find out who's in charge of what as the closing credits roll up the screen after the news. You're looking for the "Assignment Editor," the "Managing Editor," or the "News Director." If you can't catch it, call! Most likely, you'll have to call the radio stations, anyway. They generally don't announce who the editor is over the air. Don't be intimidated. Call!

## HELP FROM HOME

No matter what business you're in, you probably deal with larger business groups, suppliers, and trade associations. These contacts can come in very handy, and they can do a lot for you. Keep on your toes when looking at the information than comes from your suppliers. They are a valuable resource for information.

## PRESS INFORMATION

Most companies launch new products with a large amount of hoopla, and you should be ready to take complete advantage of it. If you happen to be a retailer, contact your wholesale distributor or your manufacturer. Odds are they have put some big bucks into a PR campaign for everything they have done since you started your business, and all of that is readily available to you: pre-printed brochures, complete and expertly assembled press information kits, video films, etc. If you happen to be in a professional practice or other business, contact your professional association or trade organization.

By contacting these people to get information you'll be accomplishing two things: You'll get the information to use effectively in your program, and you'll send a message to your suppliers and manufacturers that you're serious about making money with their products. Once you get started, you'll be amazed at how well they treat you at the home office.

Get your company and your local media on the press mailing lists of your suppliers and manufacturers. Usually, all you have to do is ask, and perhaps send them your local media list, and pretty soon your industry information will

begin appearing in your local papers without you having
to do anything. And most important, your suppliers will be
more than happy to put *your* company's name as *their*
contact in town. Again, a double dose of publicity, and all
you have to do is make a few phone calls!

## PROMOTION MONEY

Many large companies have developed what they call **co-op**
funds for their local retail outlets. These funds are primarily for advertising, but you can check to see how it works
for promotions and other special uses. The premise of
co-op funds is simple: Suppliers will pay from 50%-100%
of **your** advertising costs as long as you highlight their
products. The programs have been highly successful, and
the support they offer you is amazing. We'll get into co-op
programs in detail later.

Suppliers (through knowledge and material) can be
instrumental in making your business thrive, and they may
also pay for some of your promotional costs. For example,
one supplier may help you put together a local seminar on
their latest product. Another manufacturer may help you
with "Acme Widget Week" at your store. Only your initia-
tive will get the job done.

Key words in this chapter are simple:
**Start Thinking News!**
**Start Thinking PR Program!**
**Start!**

Public Relations is very simple, and you don't have to
have an MBA to run a successful PR program for your
company. Your company will be recognized, your employee morale will skyrocket, and the bottom line, you'll
make more money.

# CHAPTER TWO

# MEET THE PRESS
## What They Want, What They Don't Want

Members of the press are people, too. They are just like you and me. They have families, drive station wagons, and live in your town. Their job is reporting the news, just as your job is selling widgets, computer consulting, or contracting. They possess similar likes and dislikes. So, to begin, figure out what concerns you most in your business, and it is likely to concern the city editor, the business writer, the features reporter, or the real estate editor.

Generally speaking, television stations, radio stations, magazines and newspapers deal in the interesting and important aspects of the communities they serve. You and your small business don't have to be General Motors or Coca Cola to make business news. While your product or service may not be as dramatic or as revolutionary in the world's overall business picture, you've got to remember that your business has merit.

21

One reason you're in business in the first place is to actively contribute to the welfare and the economic health of your community and your profession or industry.

You may not think a story on Mr. Smith's pumpkin farm is of any earth-shattering relevance, but there are people out there who do. At least once a year, right before Halloween, you'll see a picture and a story on Mr. Smith's pumpkin farm. His product relates to a particular event during the year, but he is also a contributor to the economy of the community in his own way.

It has been said that the **average** person in this country gets his/her name in the paper three times during his/her life: when he/she is born, marries, and dies. The most important reason a newspaper has for its existence is to chronicle the daily and weekly life of its community. (Hence, the name *Chronicle* for so many newspapers in this country.) Mr. Smith's pumpkin farm is part of that life, as is your company, your staff, and your work in the community. The reason some people get their names and deeds in the paper more often than others, whether they intend it or not, is that they make it so.

Chronicling the daily life of a community is to chronicle the changes in the community. Change can mean a fire that destroyed a house, it can mean another game in the "win" column for the local high school baseball team, or it can mean the addition of a business that hasn't been in town before. Anything that changes or alters the life and routine of the community constitutes news.

You're in business because you think what you do is important. But just because you think it's important doesn't necessarily mean anyone else does. However, your business is an important part of the chronicle of your community. Through effective public relations, you can significantly increase your importance. Simply give the press what the want the way they want it.

Put yourself in the shoes of an editor. In the course of an average day, that editor receives bundles of information from hoardes of companies, politicians, associations, trade groups, and PR agencies trying to get their names/products into the paper. Even so, you have a number of advantages working for you, so don't be scared off by thinking that you're contributing to this logjam. You're just as important — if not more so — than all other others vying for the attention of the editor.

To begin with, you're local, which means you will generally have top priority over most national stuff that gets buried on the editors' desks. And provided you present your information properly, your "news" has more interest to the editor's immediate readership. Your news may even make some of that national information worth more because of your local involvement with the general issues. Even though you're competing for the editor's attention with many others who are trying the same thing, it's the information that's important. People don't get to be editors without learning to recognize what's important and what's not. Begin learning the same thing and you will begin to think like an editor.

Again, *think news.*

What does an editor put into the paper, and why does it make the front page? Page four? The keys to a story's finding a home on one of the many pages in the paper are *people* and *affect*. How many of whom does the story affect? What is its relevance to what segment of the daily life of your community, your county, your country? How will this story affect them, how has it affected them, and what kind of changes can be expected?

Let's look at a news story: the kind of news story that

---

## Hammer Tool & Die Slated For Closure

CLEVELAND - Hammer Tool & Die, a Cleveland subsidary of World Engineering, Inc., employing 530 workers, will close its doors June 10th. The company has been producing parts for the airplane industry in the Cleveland area for the past 27 years.

World Engineering, headquartered in Los Angeles, cited excessive costs in modernizing the Cleveland plant to meet the new demands in airplane construction.

"It's strictly an economic decision from the home office," said a spokesperson for World. "We will do our best to relocate as may workers as possible to our other operations."

Angry union officials of Local 215, representing over 450 of the plant's employees, emerged from an emergency meeting last night to condemn the decision.

"We have a contract, and this is all in gross violation of it," said Harry Smith, union spokesman. "We will be meeting later this week with company officials to discuss our grievances."

World has operations in Los Angeles, New York, Chicago, and Miami.

---

appears in newspapers across the country every month. Let's look at how it affects people and how it is reported.

What is this about? If you think it's about another big company shutting down another plant because it can't afford to operate it anymore, you're missing the whole story. That's only a small part of it.

This story is about people, changes, disruption, and broken promises and dreams. It's about ideas, ambitions and goals; and it embodies the hard realities of life.

It affects thousands of people around the nation. Just to name a few: every local business that supplies materials or services to the plant and those from other states and other countries who do the same; union officials in New York, Chicago and Los Angeles; all the children who will have to change schools, meet new friends, and start new lives; the hot dog vendor who has been supplying the workers lunch for the past fifteen years; the local churches, some of which may lose significant portions of their congregations; the guy at the corner deli who will miss his favorite customer every Saturday morning at 8:00 A.M. sharp; the coach of last year's championship Little League team, who is losing his star pitcher; three service stations, two car dealerships, five banks, eighteen restaurants, two restaurant supply houses, four busboys working their ways through college, and one lonely waitress who felt sorry for the drill press operator with no family. You get the idea.

Granted, closing a large plant is pretty serious stuff. But, to you, your employees, and your customers, your business is pretty important, too. Your business, no matter how big or small, affects people far and beyond those **you** can name, and then some. And, that's news.

When presenting your news, once again remember, news people get bothered enough by the professional PR jockeys with their glossy folders, flashy photos, etc.(If your closing a large plant, then by all means bother them.) The members of the media truly appreciate a simple, well-written, important news item on which *they* decide if its worth using. Not that you shouldn't follow-up with a phone call. It is important to call to see if they got your release and if they need any additional information. This helps them become more familiar with your name and your company.

But don't spend a day-and-a-half on the phone with them. Keep the conversation courteous, short and to the point. If the editor or reporter wants to ask you anything, he/she will. Remember, these people are professionals, and they know what their doing. And don't worry if they don't ask anything right away or if they seem short and impolite. People who work in this business are very busy, especially on some of the smaller papers where each reporter is covering a little of everything.

And don't forget about the deadline pressure all reporters and editors are under. This is a constant fact of life in the news business. When you call a newspaper, TV station or radio station, you will most always be interrupting something. The news never stops, and neither do those who report it.

This is why reporters and editors appreciate short and simple phone calls. You got through, they got the information, they don't need anything else now, thank you, have a nice day. **Bingo, you're done**. If they want to call you back, they will when they have a chance. If they don't, no big deal. If everything got into the newspaper that everyone wanted to see in the newspaper, there wouldn't be any trees left in Oregon.

Major newspapers and smaller newspapers print different items, the smaller newspapers tending to print the news that's more applicable to their local communities. While it is tougher to get a story into the large newspapers, don't be discouraged. In many cases, an editor will have to receive a number of news releases about your company before your news appears in one of the major metropolitan newspapers.

We'll get to writing a good press release a bit later, but as a general rule never send anything lengthy to the media. A twenty-page in-depth analysis of your industry/company won't get printed. Unless specifically asked by an editor, keep **all** press information short, basic, and to-the-point. Communicate your ideas as succinctly as possible. Don't stray. Just state the facts: who, what, where, why, when, and how.

If your news is that one of your employees set a sales record, say that. Don't go into how your company is on the verge of creating a revolutionary new product that will change the world as we know it. That's for another time.

News people want news. The exact definition of news is subject to hours of debate. Suffice it to say that there are such thing as slow news days. You easily recognize one the moment your local anchor introduces a story about bugs and the adverse effects they have on your windshield. Realistically, you don't know what exactly will make news until you give it a shot. However, use just a few principles in this little book, and you're sure to stack the deck in your favor.

Basically, there are two kinds of news: the news that happens — plane crashes, volcano eruptions, earthquakes — and news that's created — legislation, corporate events, sports, etc. You are making news happen, and you will create the events that will appear in the media. (Key: You will be creating news, not fabricating news. Big difference, and don't forget it!) You're creating news by being in business, and you create news each day you stay in business.

Let's create some news the way the press wants it.

Halloween is a time of year that's supposed to be fun for kids and adults alike. Yet, scares of candy-poisoning, etc., have left many parents afraid to let their children venture out into the dark of the night. For promotional purposes, many companies have been offering "safe" Halloween coupons to be redeemed later at the particular retailers store. It's an excellent promotional item, and it serves the trick-or-treating children well. Yet, more and more companies every year seem to be jumping on the safe-Halloween bandwagon.

A former client of mine, a housing developer, wanted something a bit more intricate and unique for the company's Halloween promotions. My job was to sell homes to the outlying community, and we had been highlighting the development's image as a safe, homey neighborhood. We wanted to keep that theme. But, we didn't want to waste anyone's time with a gimmicky promotional stunt.

After looking around the development itself, we noticed that all of the model homes were in clusters of five or six, and all were in walking distance of each other. Bingo! We promoted an old-fashioned Halloween — kids walking from home to home, many with their parents, and getting candy at the doors of all the model homes. They got real candy — that we had inspected in advance — and not coupon books. Each builder in the development eagerly participated. Their sales staffs dressed in costumes on Halloween night, and the went all-out decorating their homes with pumpkins, skeletons, etc.

The event served several purposes: 1) It allowed parents to feel safe about their children going door-to-door in a safe environment; 2) the children had an "old-fashioned" Halloween, fun, safe, and filled with enthusiastic people; 3) the event generated a great deal of good, image-enhancing publicity for the developer and the individual homebuilders; 4) many children came with their parents, so the individual homebuilders even sold a few new homes as a result of the visits to their models. In other words, the event was unique to our community, and not just another gimmick to get news. (See Chapter Four for details on this particular promotion.)

You get the idea. News is everywhere, and you make some of it. In many instances you do it without realizing it, but no one may know unless you tell them about it. The members of the press are just like you and me, and you are important to them. Use all your advantages, and get used to their terms and the way they operate. Keep your news short and to the point, just as you do your conversations with the media. And, again, and I'll stress this at the end of each chapter, **THINK NEWS!**

# CHAPTER 3

# HOW TO WRITE A GOOD PRESS RELEASE
## Be Your Own Reporter

The press release is your main weapon in the war of business news. Done correctly and packaged properly, it will get you the attention you need to be more successful in your business.

The press release is your prime link with the media. It is how you let them know what you're doing. The press release the editors want allows them to sit at their desks, scan it quickly, judge its merits as a news item, and use it or toss it. Simple. (Golden rule of media relations and life in general: *The simpler it is, the better it works*.) Keep things simple, and make life as easy as possible for the editors.

There is no tremendous magic to writing a press release. It's one of the simplest forms of written communication.

## Build a Good Press Release

A good press release has its roots in the words of the immortal Sgt. Joe Friday — "Just the facts, ma'am." That's exactly how a good press release is written: just the facts organized concisely in the order of their importance. Skip the antiquated cliche's, outmoded adjectives, and glowing embellishments. Real life and PR: the simpler they are the better they work.

A friend of mine at the *Los Angeles Times* reviews his daily crop of releases and laughs out loud. A real estate release once described a master bedroom as "something that would make Valentino swoon." This is serious trash-can liner, and that's right where absurd adjectives and bizarre embellishments go.

The basic structure of a press release should mirror that of the news story., This structure is what journalists call the Inverted Pyramid. All news stories, with the exception of lengthy features, are written this way. (See Diagram.)

**THE INVERTED PYRAMID**

SUMMARY LEAD PARAGRAPH
Who, What, Where, Why, When & How

SECOND PARAGRAPH
Most important elements of story
—regardless of chronological order

DETAILS
In descending
order
of importance

The primary pertinent information is contained in the first paragraph of the story, otherwise known as the lead. The editor, like his readers, should be able to read the lead paragraph of any story and know exactly what the story is about. (*Who*, *what*, *where*, *why*, *when*, and *how*.)

At this point, the reader makes the decision whether to read on and get the details or skip it and move his or her attention to another story. Whether you realize it or not, this is the way most of us read the morning paper.

This basic structure of a news story has been around since the dawn of the modern newspaper age decades ago. It was designed so that it could be lopped off at the bottom. The information in a news story begins with the most important facts and descends to the least important facts. If the person who is laying out the paper runs out of room on a particular page, he can just cut out the last paragraph (or five) without damaging the essential parts of the story.

Now that you've begun thinking news a little more each day, start reading the paper and watching you're evening local newscast more thoroughly. Pick up on the trends and notice the aspects and angles that allow an event, an idea, or a happening to become news. And don't forget radio. Tune in your car radio to your local talk/news station and listen to it.

Virtually every guest on every talk show got there through a public relations effort. It's not hard to get on the radio. Even though you're promoting something, you and your event are a happening news event. And with more and more hours of talk to fill, pointing out your interesting items to a talk show producer is not only accepted, it is encouraged and appreciated. And be it radio, TV, or newspaper, each appreciates the same form of press release.

We discussed the inverted pyramid as standard journalistic practice. Now, let's examine a few basic press releases and we'll trace a few common threads so we can build our own.

Release 1 is the release I sent when I first went into business. It didn't matter that I was working with a small computer, a desk and a telephone out of the spare bedroom in my apartment. I had a public relations practice, I needed the money, and I wanted the world to know it. I wasn't employing gobs of people, and I wasn't pumping tons of money into the economy at that moment. However, I was going to have an impact on the business community, and that's news. I received a nice announcement in both local papers.

This release is simple, short and to the point. It's not an advertisement, just a straightforward business announcement. (Anything remotely resembling an advertisement will become trash-can liner.)

## SLUG LINES

Write all your releases on your own stationery and follow the standard form in this example. Put the date, the place from where the news originates ("News from HILL*TOP Co."), and the release date (when the news will be news — "For Immediate Release"). You have just composed what are known as slug lines, and they provide the editors with a quick reference to your news item.

Nearly everything you write will be slugged "For Immediate Release," although you may have something timed for release at a later date. In this case, you would slug it for release on a specific date. For example: "FOR RELEASE: Tuesday, January 5th, 1991." But, always try to slug "For Immediate Release," because this allows the editor to use your item at his or her discretion.

4/17/89                                    **ACME**

NEWS FROM HILL*TOP Co.              **NURSERIES**

FOR IMMEDIATE RELEASE                    **Address**

### FORMER BUSINESS EDITOR STARTS
### HILL*TOP PUBLIC RELATIONS

The former editor of Business Quarterly Magazine, Dennis
C. Hill, has established a public relations practice in
Colorado Springs. Mr. Hill will be handling media/pub-
lic/community relations and other services for clients in
Colorado Springs and the Southwest United States.

Hill, a resident of Colorado Springs for two years,
attended Northern Arizona University and Arizona State
University, studying courses in several major fields. He
has been involved in various projects in Colorado Springs
including serving as Vice-President and Director of Public
Relations for NOVA Technological Center, a 1,100 acre
business park adjacent to the Consolidated Space Operations
Center (CSOC). He went on to serve as Editor in Chief of
Business Quarterly.

Hill began his career with the Hudson Register-Star,
Hudson, NY, in 1973, and he has been involved with various
publications ever since. His new firm, HILL*TOP Company,
is located at 1202 E. San Miguel, Suite #1, Colorado Springs,
CO 80909. Their telephone number is (303) 555-2859.

                        --30--

For Further Information:

Dennis C. Hill

HILL*TOP Co.

1202 E. San Miguel #1

Colorado Springs, CO 80909

(303) 555-2859

**Release 1**

## THE HEADLINE

The headline follows the slug lines, and it is the second point of quick reference for the editor. This is where you need to grab the editor's attention, but not be so creative that you get corny. A headline on a press release should tell the story in just a few words. Look at these headlines:

> "ACME DESIGNS WIDGET
>
> "SMITH TO RUN FINANCE DEPARTMENT"
>
> "JONES CORP. MOVES OFFICES"

These headlines get the point across, but they're boring. You want the editor to read on, so you don't stall him or her with a snoozy headline. Try these:

> "ACME'S WIDGET SPEEDS PERFORMANCE"
>
> "FORMER CHASE VP TO RUN FINANCE DEPARTMENT"
>
> "RAPID GROWTH FORCES JONES CORP.
> TO LARGER QUARTERS"

There are reasons for everything you do in business, so spell those reasons out briefly in the headline of every release you send. In the same way that a sign in front of your store forces people to look at it, a good headline will force the editor's attention toward it. Practice writing headlines while just walking around your office or store. (Think headlines. Think action. Practice on the silly things that happen in your everyday life.)

> "COFFEE MACHINE OVERFILL
> SENDS SECRETARY AFLUTTER"
>
> "TOP SALESMAN SETS RECORD:
> CREDITS NEW GOLD TOOTH"
>
> "NEW PENCIL SHARPENER LOCATION
> IMPROVES TRAFFIC"

Action! Action in every headline everywhere! You get the idea.

**"LITTLE BILLY'S HOMER SEND TEAM TO PLAYOFFS"**
**"RUNNY YOLKS IGNITE BREAKFAST FRACAS"**
**"WIFE TIRES OF HEADLINES: PACKS BAGS"**

## THE LEAD

Now that you've got the editor's attention, you need to construct a good lead. You don't have to be Ernest Hemingway to write a press release, and you need not have worked a lifetime at *The New York Times* to put together a good lead paragraph. A good lead paragraph will get you into the paper, mentioned on the radio, or talked about on TV.

Remember: *All releases are double-spaced!* This gives the editors room to cross out your phrases, replace your words, re-arrange your sentences, and basically make a mess of all your hard work. Don't fret; editors have been doing it to the best writers throughout history. It's their job.

A good lead paragraph should concisely tell the whole story in one or two sentences. Nothing fancy, but the action in your lead is the reason for your release. Look at the following lead:

```
John Smith was put in charge of the
fern department at Acme Nurseries
Thursday. He was formerly in the plant
food department, where he worked for
15 years.
```

It's not overly exciting. Clean, good, and surely passable. But, let's liven it up a bit.

```
John Smith was named Manager of Acme
Nurseries 1500-plant fern department
Thursday, according to Eli Jones Gen-
eral Manager. Smith brings with him a
```

    15-year background of technical knowl-
    edge in plant health, having special-
    ized in plant foods and vitamins.

A little spice makes a world of difference. In this new version, we've identified the large selection of plants Acme offers, specified Mt. Smith's knowledge of his business, and acknowledged his lengthy career in the industry. Note the credit line — "According to..." It's important to credit someone whenever possible; crediting someone with providing the information has more credibility than Mr. Smith simply appearing on the page as manager of the fern department. Also, from a libel standpoint, editors like to have someone other than themselves and their reporters accountable for what goes in their newspapers.

Please note "15." In 1975 the Associated Press put together *The Associated Press Stylebook and Libel Manual*, which is the journalist's "Bible," published by Addison-Wesley. Buy the latest edition of it. It is from this manual that we know to spell out number one through nine and all numbers that begin a sentence. The book is filled with all sorts of tips on style, and it will give you tremendous insight into your morning newspaper. It will also help you with any peculiar questions you may have regarding your own press releases that aren't covered in this book. Remember, we're trying to give the press what they want the way they want it. (By the way, in this book you often see the numbers one through ninety-nine spelled out. Book editors use a different "Bible." So unless you're writing a book stick with the one through nine rule.)

Most press releases you will write will be no more than one or two pages. It is not always possible, but try to keep them that way. As I said earlier, if the editor wants more, he'll let you know.

Like any essay, the paragraphs that follow your lead

will both support and add information to your lead. Again thinking news and looking for a unique angle for his story, let's get back to Mr. Smith and his ferns.

Has he won any awards? Agricultural prizes? Did he develop any special plant food that won him recognition in the botanical world? Has he studied anywhere? Any college degrees that relate to what he's doing now? Or, does he have college degrees that have absolutely nothing to do with what he's doing now? Did he grow up in a rural area? Downtown Manhattan?

Ask enough questions, and you're bound to find that unique angle that will sell your story to an editor. For the sake of this chapter, let's just say that Mr. Smith grew up in the heart of a big city and never saw a fern until he and his wife took a summer vacation in South America. (Great for your follow-up call: "Yea! The guy never saw a blade of grass until he was thirty!")

## 2nd PARAGRAPH

```
Smith, a Brooklyn, NY, native, holds
an M.B.A. from Harvard. He hadn't
thought about a career in plant man-
agement until he developed a keen
interest in the subject one summer
thirty years ago in South America.
```

Now we've got the editor. By now, he's wondering what a guy with an MBA is doing schlepping fern food from plant to plant and why the guy was in South America. If it's interesting to the editor, he'll want it for his readers.

Our next paragraph would be a good time for a quote from Mr. Smith, backing up the second paragraph. Quotes are important, especially to a newspaper. They go one step beyond "According to..." and they add even more credibility to the story. Editors need quotes. They're official, stamped in stone. There is no refuting a direct quote. Now, if this were going to be a basic "JOHN SMITH AP-POINTED FERN MANAGER" story, we probably wouldn't use any. But, we're trying to breathe some life into John Smith and Acme's ferns. (A note about quotes: Always consult with John Smith — or whomever you are quoting — about what he or she is going to say.)

### 3rd PARAGRAPH

"I never thought about a career in plants until my wife and I went rafting one summer in Peru," said Smith. "We were paddling through a rain forest one afternoon, and I noticed all the plant life surrounding me. From then on, I was hooked."

### 4th PARAGRAPH

Smith has worked for Acme Nurseries for 15 years. Acme is located at 35 Main St. in downtown Denver.

This is your basic press release. When you put the whole thing together it should look like Release 2.

Note the "--30--" at the end of this release. In the old days when the telegraphers used to send a story over the wire, "30" was their signal that they had completed their transmission. It's still used today in the business, and you may use it to signal the end of your press releases. (You can also use "###" at the end of your release, but I prefer "--30--" for reasons strictly nostalgic.)

Always give your name as a contact with your address and telephone number following the release itself. This is

4/17/89

NEWS FROM HILL*TOP Co.

FOR IMMEDIATE RELEASE

**Phone**

## ACME
## NURSERIES
**35 Main St.**
**Denver, Colorado 80123**

### PLANT EXPERT NAMED ACME MANAGER:
### CREDITS RAFT EXPLORATION

John Smith was named manager of Acme Nurseries' 1500-plant fern department Thursday, according to Eli Jones, General Manager. Smith brings with him a 15-year background of technical knowledge in plant health, having specialized in plant foods and vitamins.

Smith, a Brooklyn, NY, native, holds an M.B.A. from Harvard. He hadn't thought about a career in plant management until he developed a keen interest in the subject one summer 30 years ago in South America.

"I never thought about a career in plants until my wife and I went rafting one summer in Peru," said Smith. "We were paddling through a rain forest one afternoon, and I noticed all the plant life surrounding me. From then on I was hooked."

Smith has worked for Acme Nursery for 15 years. Acme is located at 35 Main St. in downtown Denver.

--30--

For Further Information:

Eli Jones, General Manager

Acme Nurseries

35 Main St.

Denver, Colorado 80123

(303) 555-1234

**Release 2**

important, if you expect to get a call from an editor who wants more information. Your contact lines are especially important when you deal with television and radio stations. They may need to contact you for filming and interviews.

## PHOTOS THAT WORK

The guidelines for good photos that should get into the paper are simple. Unless specifically requested, all photos you will send will be in black and white. Even though many papers are using color on the front pages, this space is usually reserved for their own photographers or photos from the national wire services. All inside pages are still all black and white.

Photo's should be processed into 5" x 7" or 8" x 10" prints. Since your photo will rarely appear in the paper in its actual size, these two sizes give an editor plenty of room to work with. Your best bet is to find a photo lab that will make you a contact sheet. A contact sheet inexpensively displays all your photos on one page, and you can pick and choose the ones you want. It saves a fortune in processing costs. Now, with a contact sheet, your photos will be the same size as the negative, and some of them may be a bit fuzzy. Not to worry. The contact sheet is meant to give you the idea of what's in the photos. Corrections can be made when the actual photo is printed.

Your photos should actually be a bit dull; not fuzzy, mind you, but not glossy with a whole lot of contrast. If you look very closely, perhaps under a magnifying glass, you'll see that the photos that appear on the pages of your morning newspaper are not really photos at all. The are a series of dots. The darker the image, the closer together the dots; the lighter the image in the photo, the farther apart the dots. To help insure clarity in the photos that eventually appear in the paper, you need a fairly flat (not glossy) image.

Your photos need to focus on two key items: action and people. A sales photo of a new machine does nothing. A photo of a machine that is moving, spitting out sparks, copies, or whatever, with a man or woman working with it is much more likely to get published. Examine the photos on the following pages, and you'll note the differences. As always, check the paper to see what's getting published and what's not.

david bradley
Sebastian, Florida
(305) 589-1236

If you know someone famous, or you can wrangle your way into becoming the **official** supplier, photographer, distributor, or consultant to anyone or anything famous that would help promote you and your identity, do it as it fits your image.

Plaque, check, or award presentations are always good and almost always well received. Whenever you honor someone in the community, or you or a member of your firm is honored, it's worth a photo. Always be sure to include the name of your company, the positions and titles of all involved.

This is a good, though fairly standard, photo. While this doesn't look like a whole lot of action is in this photo, it represents people working on a project that is happening. People will want to know what is being built, where it's going to be built, and when it will be finished.

Celebrities make news wherever they go, and they are especially valuable in small towns. Politics aside, look at the image this photo stands for: conservative America with flag, celebrity, and you.

This is an advertising photo. There's no action, and unless the story behind it is something truly incredible, this photo will **not** make it through the story process.

Even though there is a celebrity in the photo, this shot is useless for some obvious reasons.

This is a standard mug shot with a twist. You will need one of these for each new person who joins your firm, and you can keep it on file for each time they make the news. Dressing appropriately adds to this photo tremendously.

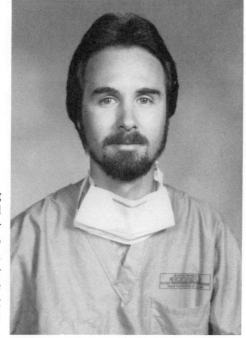

The celebrity in this photo should have been centered with the eagle and "Presidency" in the background above his head.

This photo is more likely to be printed in the newspaper, although it would accomplish more with the eagle in the background as in the previous photo.

Captions are always taped to the back of any photos you send. Captions are simple to write. Who is doing what with which? Period. Your press release will tell everyone what they need to know.

## PACKAGING YOUR EFFORT

Standard releases with no photos or diagrams can be put into an envelope (your company stationary, of course) and sent off. If you enclose a photo, diagram, or anything that can't be folded, use a folder. It's best if you have your own made, but since we're trying to save you money, just go to the drug store and grab some colorful student folders. I've found that these work well: they stand out on the editor's desk. Glue your business card in the center of the folder, and don't forget to remove the price tag. When you open the folder, everything you have done should be on the right-hand side.

Even if you've talked to an editor just once, paper-clip a small note to the outside of the folder. "Bob, thought you might be interested in this. Call me if you have any questions. D.C." Even if you don't know him, he just may rack his brain trying to remember you.

Send all press releases first-class mail. The money you just saved on folders will make up for the postage. You want the release to get where it's going, so spring for the extra postage. It's worth it.

There are all sorts of theories on the best day for your release to arrive on the editor's desk. Don't worry about it. Any day but Monday is a good day. Even if it arrives on a Monday, it may be put aside until later in the week.

Now that you're in a program, have learned about the media, and know how to write a press release, it's time to enter the wonderful world of promotion. Don't let anything scare you. You're thinking news, now let's make some!

# CHAPTER 4

# THE PRESS CONFERENCE
## Your Day in The Sun

The press conference is your chance to shine for all the world to see. Don't get nervous...yet.

Press conferences can take many forms and they can be held for many reasons. As a general rule, they are reserved for significant announcements, but no law says you can't use a press conference to make your news more interesting. Try not to think of it in the traditional sense of the press conference. We all see politicians in front of a hundred microphones taped together at a podium. This, in so many cases, is simply not exciting. Reporters go to those types of conferences because they have to. You want the press to show up at yours because they want to be there.

Press conferences are your chance to get as creative as you can — without getting corny. There's nothing worse than a dull press conference, or a press conference where nothing happens.

A press conference is designed for the media, and it's

your job to inform and entertain them. The very best conferences, the ones that entertain the media enough to get on the six and eleven o'clock news, involve some sort of hands-on activity. We'll get to this in a few moments.

*Don't be intimidated.*

We've already established that you are news and that what you do is important in the overall scheme of things. And, please, don't think you have to be Donald Trump, George Bush, or the CEO of IBM (or their press agents) to call a press conference.

The press conference is a special event. Like all other special events, it should be thought of as a party. The preparations are similar, from the invitations to the refreshments and the show, which is you, your company and your news.

## ORGANIZATION AND ENTERTAINMENT

Organization is the key to staging a successful press conference. Think *staged* and you'll do just fine. Pretend you're throwing a party for a few exclusive guests.

Advance work is your most important task in all areas of PR. Organized preparation and attention to the details will tell the press a lot about you and a lot about the way you run your business. In outlining the details of a press conference, follow the following steps. After all, you don't want to throw a party where nobody shows.

### Step 1 — Date, Time and Place

You should plan a press conference as far in advance as possible. The only instance in which you would call one on the spur of the moment is in the event of an emergency (See Chapter Seven) or if the announcement simply can't wait. You have to judge that one on your own.

A week's notice is usually plenty of time, but be sure to

check your local paper's calendar of events section. You don't want to announce a new line of revolutionary computers on the same morning as the space shuttle passes through your home town. You want a fairly clean news slate for the day of your announcement, and even then there's no guarantee that anyone will show up. (I learned this one the hard way. I once scheduled a press conference at the grand opening of a new boat dealership on the same morning the dictator of Nicaragua arrived at the airport to speak at a local university. Guess where the press wasn't.)

The date, time and place of your press conference depend on your reasons for holding the press conference to begin with. As a rule, **NEVER ON MONDAY**, for the same reasons you really wouldn't want any extra work on Monday: you're waking up from the weekend, you're bummed because you have to go back to work, etc. Thursday is pretty busy for the newspaper folks, only because much of the Saturday and Sunday sections are put together on Thursday. Other than those, all other days are pretty much the same. The press is always busy.

When it comes to picking a place for your press conference, use what you have. No law requires you to lease the local press room (the place where many of your town's PR agencies like to call gatherings of the press); and, in fact, you'll probably never want to do that. Dull, dull, dull! Tie it into what you're doing. Lawyers — use an empty courtroom. Consultants — use one of your more successful projects. Financial planners — aboard a yacht (doesn't have to be yours necessarily). Writers — try the local library. Artists, try the local museum. Opening a new restaurant? VIP press dinner, free of charge, of course. You get the idea. Use what you've got. If you don't happen to have it on hand, find it. You attract attention by being creative and by having something important to say. Now's your chance to get as creative as you can.

New businesses can always hold one at their places of business. That's where you'll want the media to focus it's attention most of the time anyway.

If your announcement/news has something to do with an event, you'll want to hold your press conference before the event. If your news is simply news, it's your job to create an event around your news to make it more exciting.

For example, if you're introducing a new line of widgets in the fall, play off of what you have. Dress up for Halloween. Serve a small turkey to the press if your announcement falls around Thanksgiving. Have a giant leaf raking contest if the leaves are falling.

### Step 2 — The Media/Press Kit

The media kit is what you will hand the press when they come to your press conference. It basically reiterates what you tell them at the press conference. The media kit should contain the following:

1. A press release recapping what you plan to announce at the conference

2. Any applicable photos of whatever you are announcing or introducing

3. A copy of the statement you will read to the media gathered

4. Any applicable promotional material that may pertain to what you're doing

5. If you can swing it, some sort of specialty gift with your logo on it (This is very optional, and it can get expensive. Save this for something important. Save it for when you're making money.)

6. Always include a business card!

If you have your own folders printed with your company name and logo on them, use these for your press kit. Just type a neat-looking label that says *Press Kit* and stick it on the upper right hand corner of each folder. If you don't have your own folders, use the colored folders we spoke about earlier.

Since you'll be greeting at the door, be sure to hand each guest a copy of the press kit the moment you say hello. This will give them a chance to look over your information; and more important, it will keep them busy while waiting for their colleagues to show up.

**Step 3 — Media Invitations**

In most cases, you don't pick up the phone and say, "Hey guys, we're having a press conference! Come on down! Make up an invitation. You can have them printed, or you can use your company letterhead for them.

Briefly outline what you plan to discuss, and always indicate what special hands-on activities you'll have available for the press to sink their cameras and tape recorders into.

Try to hand-deliver these invitations just to make sure they get where they need to go on time, and always try to find some little specialty item to go along with them. For example, I've used everything from gift-wrapped Halloween candy for a Halloween promotion to model airplane paperweights for an aviation fair.

These little items are attention-getters. They get your invitations opened. They can get expensive, so use your own judgement.

The day before the press conference, make your confirmation calls. Just call the papers, radio stations, and TV stations to make sure they're coming. "Hi, this is Al down at Acme Computers. I'm just calling to make sure you'll be at the press conference for our new line of computers that do everything from starting your car in the morning to actually paying your taxes. Right. Tomorrow at four. Thank you." Simple enough.

## Step 4 — Staging Your conference

Setting up a press conference is like organizing your daughter's sixth birthday party. Many reporters hate press conferences. And after chasing down stories all day, they truly appreciate a little fun and excitement. Give it to them.

Now that you have a place for your press conference, you need to arrange a staging area. The trick here is to arrange an area for **MPO** — Maximum-Photo-Opportunity. Your stage set is designed for the TV cameras and the newspaper photographers. You want your company's name/logo in every lens present. Chairs for the reporters should be available, and there should be a clearing in the middle for the TV camera crews. (A camera crew these days is usually just one husky guy/girl loaded down with wires, microphones, and battery packs.) You may not need a podium, but you might want to have some sort of a table for your notes.

You'll need a refreshment table, which is never optional. Members of the press are always on the run, and they rarely have a chance to eat anything of real substance. They *always* appreciate a snack or anything remotely resembling such: coffee, juice and donuts in the morning, some small sandwiches and sodas after 11:30 A.M. Ice water is always mandatory.

(When you start making money, you might arrange for a luncheon press conference. They can be done relatively inexpensively if you and your staff handle all the preparations. You might want to save the fancy stuff for when you announce that your company is going public. Then, you can have it catered, with waiters, etc.)

This sort of attention to detail adds to the overall impression the press will have when they walk away. You want them to leave totally satisfied. You want the front page and the evening news.

You will be the focus of attention while you're speaking and answering questions, but make sure that what you're announcing — an exciting new product, a trailblazing new piece of machinery or equipment, or an unbelievable new employee — is close enough to be very visible when the cameras are pointed at you.

If it's a product you're announcing, demonstrate it! Afterward, let members of the press play with it. Get them involved. (Make sure to try it out yourself a few times in advance to make sure it works and that you know how to work the thing. If you can't figure it out, have someone there who does. There's nothing more embarrassing than standing behind a great product that doesn't work with the world watching. Remember when John Cameron Swayze, the venerable spokesman for Timex watches, attached a watch to the propeller of an outboard motor on live television? The engine cranked up its horsepower, and when it stopped, the watch couldn't be found. It had been ground to bits. Dry runs are crucial.)

Always dress appropriately for the press. Appropriate costumes add a good light dimension to any event. But, if it's a serious announcement, stick to jackets and ties, skirts and blouses.

Your statement should be relatively short and simple. What are you announcing? How does it affect who, and why? And what kind of changes can be expected because of this announcement/product? Done. Then open the floor for any questions.

Answer questions in a forthright, honest manner. Smile, and always look at the reporter asking the question. Simple, straightforward answers do the job. If you don't know the answer to a question, *never* make something up. Do the best you can. Just be honest.

Unless you've poked a massive hole in Einstein's Theory of Relativity and have a lot of technical explanation, call a halt to the conference within a half-hour. Thank the press for coming and mention that you will be available for individual interviews and questions immediately. These "stand-ups" are important, because they give the individual members of the press a chance to hold one-on-one interviews with you.

## ENTERTAINING THE PRESS

Staging a press conference is like staging a show. That's really what you're doing. Go all out! Just watch boxing promoter Don King announce a fight sometime. It's a spectacle! Action is the key at any press conference. The press lives for action, so make it interesting for them. In turn they will make it even more interesting for their readers, viewers and listeners.

It's OK to get carried away at a press conference. In some cases, the more you get carried away, the more the press will enjoy it.

For example, we once promoted an aviation festival. No big deal as these things go. However, we had to attract thousands of people to make money for the non-profit group sponsoring the event. (Non-profit causes and associations — like small businesses — have little money.)

You could fit the entire media budget on the head of a pin. So, the majority of the attention we would get would come from the initial press conference. We had to make it spectacular using what we had.

We obtained permission to stage the conference on the tarmac of the private jet hanger at our local airport. We set up coffee and donuts inside the hanger, and arranged the chairs and speakers table outside near the taxiway and runway. Surrounding the conference area and right behind the speakers', we placed several of the antique airplanes that would be at the show.

All this preparation established an exciting atmosphere for the conference itself. This was staging. The press showed up in full force because we offered them and their camera people rides in the old planes. We made sure to announce the rides in the press invitations. It was fun and exciting. Consequently, we got incredible coverage in all media. (They also got a chance to stock up on their aerial file footage.)

This is what I mean by entertaining the media by using what you have. In this case, we didn't have any money, but we did have airplanes, pilots, and some time. We created a series of additives to a basic press conference to make it more attractive to all media. Many press conferences are boring as hell; but if you surround the conference with incentives to make it more fun for the press, they're much more likely to attend. If they have a great time, your odds of increased publicity are drastically improved. So use your imagination!

One final note:

Don't worry if the press doesn't show up in force. There really are times when more important news happens and reporters may have to cover something else. But, if you follow the above steps, use your imagination, and rally think entertainment, you shouldn't have any problem getting the press to attend.

And, don't forget about the thank you. Again, **Details** are the key to almost everything you do in PR.

# Chapter 5

# Staging A Successful Promotion
## Secure Your Identity

The promotion is our honest attempt to affect people, and this is how we make news. The men and women on this earth create the news — sometimes unintentionally, but most of the time on purpose. The promotion is the life's blood of so much of what we do in PR.

Promotions are a fact of everyday life. Nowadays, it seems every company is linking itself with a cause, a charitable effort, or a tournament of some kind. "Official" Olympic sponsors pay serious dollars to get their companies' names identified with the games. Holiday promotions by the thousands come around every Thanksgiving, Christmas, Halloween; greeting card manufacturers go nuts at everything from Mother's Day to Secretary's and Grandparent's Days.

There are events such as "National Ice Cream Week" and "National Pizza Week." In 1976 America put on one of its biggest promotions — The Bicentennial. Major film studios don't let a day pass without some sort of "blockbusting" event announcing the release of a new film.

It's called "creating news value," and the primary way we create news value is through the promotion. The successful promotion involves everything you've learned up to now: press releases, follow-ups, press conferences, how to behave with the press, what to say, etc. Now we put it all together and make it work.

The promotion is one of your most effective tools, and like the press conference, it should be thought of as a party. Only this time, the guest list is more extensive — the media, your market and the community. In effect, the press conference was your daughter's sixth birthday party. The promotion is her sixteenth. You've got to make a bigger splash to make her happy, and you've got to think about a few more details.

There are a million different kinds of promotions and as many reasons for having them. The bottom line in your business is to sell your products or services to make money. Forget for a moment what anyone told you (including me) about the intrinsic value and satisfaction of being in business. If you're not making money, all that satisfaction B.S. is moot.

This is where public relations and a good PR promotion can accomplish your goals. (Notice I didn't say PR goals, I said your goals.)

## THINK IDENTITY

One of the key accomplishments of a good overall PR program is the creation of an identity for your company. For what and in what light do you want your company to be known? Of course you want the best image possible, but you also want this image to match the identity you choose for your company. Public relations goes beyond having and maintaining a "good" image. It continually defines and refines your image.

For example: You own a small real estate firm, but you want to specialize in only the most exclusive and expensive houses in your area. Your image is fostered in everything you do, from the caliber of the people you hire and the way they dress and behave to the type of advertising you do, the kind of cars you drive, the location of your office, and the charities with which you align your firm, right down to which political party functions you attend. Each of these elements combines with the others to create your identity.

A well-timed, well-designed and well-executed promotion sells more products because it enhances your identity. So have a clear definition in your own mind as to what your company's identity should be.

Choosing a corporate identity is like choosing a suit. You're choosing to make a statement about your company. And, like buying a suit, you want it to fit well. It should be just the right color to enhance your features, and it should be of a material, cut and style that tells the world what kind of person you want them to think you are.

Unfortunately, most owner/operators of small businesses don't think about their corporate identities too much. These usually just evolve as extensions of the owners' personalities. So think about how you want to be perceived by your market and your community, and we'll design a promotion to begin linking your identity with your company.

You want an image of security and success right off the bat. Hence, you're not just a business, you're "consulting practice." You're not a wholesaler, you're a "wholesale distribution center." You're not a shoe store, you're a "fine footwear salon." You want a festive image, you stage festive promotions. You want a more subdued image, you sponsor golf clinics, not pro wrestling bouts. You want a community service image, you organize a fund drive for a local charity. You get the idea.

It is just as important to avoid those events or elements of events that *oppose* your identity. The event should be appropriate. For example, a stockbroker promoting security might not want to hold an open house on October 19th (the anniversary of the 1987 crash). A tavern owner ought not promote against drunk driving using a spokesperson who has been arrested three times for DUI. (Unless he or she has publicly reformed, etc.)

As I said, pretty obvious stuff, but you don't want to be standing around on the day of your big promotion, all of a sudden slap yourself in the forehead and say, "Oh no! Do you know what today is?" Or, "Do you know what happened today?" Or, "We can't promote this with that, so and so just got out of prison!"

## THE EFFECTIVE PROMOTION

Remember, you're planning your daughter's sixteenth birthday. And, as in any party, the ingredients in a successful promotion are:

1. Is the event timely? Does it really **mean something** to you and your targets? How is it like you and the image/identity you want to create for your business?

2. Attention to details. Once you have everything down, is everything being taken care of?

3. Organization. Is each facet of your promotion organized well? Is too much going on at once? Not enough? (The best promotions are single-theme. The more

involved you get, the more complicated it is for you and your market. Keep it simple.)

We begin creating a promotion by generating ideas. These ideas result from a brainstorming session in which we list every idea we can possibly create for any particular promotion, no matter how stupid they may seem at the time. And, believe me, a lot of them will seem dumb. However, write down every one of those ideas, and select the best of them. An idea that may seem ridiculous at the time may actually have some merits you could use.

A good brainstorming session is self perpetuating: by fostering an atmosphere of ideas, you will invariably come up with more ideas.

Try this:

If you have several other people and a chalkboard (pen and paper will also do nicely), you're in business. If you're by yourself, sit alone in a quiet atmosphere and begin to think of ideas.

Again, it doesn't matter what they are, or even if they necessarily relate. Just think ideas, ideas, ideas. If you can assemble a group of people, make sure they know that it doesn't matter what they are thinking, or why. Their ideas are supposed to roll off their tongues. Kick it off by volunteering a few bizarre ideas of your own to make sure they understand.

The emphasis is to create, not analyze. The minute you begin to analyze — as in, "No, that won't work because..." — you defeat the whole purpose of a good brainstorming session.

When you begin to run out of ideas, you will notice a definite lag in the proceedings, even if you're by yourself. When you seem to have extracted all you can from yourself and/or the group, change the emphasis.

Now you can begin to eliminate the ideas that are really off the wall, but not before you have examined why they are absurd or why they won't work.

You're fostering a positive attitude, so take all these ideas and work with them. Don't eliminate an idea until you have thought about its best characteristics, examined it on its own, combined it with others, and rolled over in our mind(s) all the reasons it will or won't work. This is an exercise in creative thinking, and it is the best way to foster ideas.

Now that you've gone through these ideas and selected the best, you can start planning your promotion. What kind of a promotion will it be, what are its goals, and how long will it last?

Now, let's walk through a promotion my firm actually did. Then I'll show you how to design your own. This promotion involves everything you may have to consider at some point or another in your own promotions.

We chose to run the Halloween promotion for a housing developer over two days, culminating with the house-to-house trick-or-treating at our model homes.

The segments were as follows: During the days, we dressed up volunteers in penguin suits and named them each "Peter Penguin." We sent them to all the local day care centers and elementary schools handing out candy and safety tips to all the children. Halloween evening we sponsored the trick-or-treating at all the model homes. It ideally linked to the identity we were trying to build, which was along the "cozy, safe, friendly neighborhood" lines.

Our program for the event went something like this:

1) We notified the individual homebuilders of our plan about two weeks in advance to give them time to think about how they would decorate their model homes, which salespersons would be in which models, what costumes the salespersons would wear, etc.

2) We sent press releases about our events and programs to the media one week in advance. One release explained Peter Penguin, and the other outlined our Trick-or-Treat tour of the model homes. They were hand-delivered with a small box of Halloween candy to members of the media most likely to cover the story. We sent one to the lifestyle/family editor, one to the real estate editor, one to the business editor, and one to the editor of the calendar of events section. This insured coverage in at least one of the sections. We included a camera-ready (ready to be printed in the newspaper — also know as a PMT or Velox) map of all the homesites with directions from all major streets.

3) We printed inexpensive flyers and hired school kids to distribute them door-to-door throughout the neighborhoods.

4) Two weeks prior to the event, we called the local radio station and arranged for a guest appearance for one of the developers on the local morning talk show.

5) We placed a small newspaper ad that ran

for three days before Halloween. The ad
was the same as the flyer.

6) We sent a short letter to one of the local TV
stations suggesting that our event on
Halloween would be just ideal for a live
remote broadcast. This substituted for any
press conference we might have had, and it
guaranteed us TV coverage.

7) Each release and arrangement with the
media included a follow-up call to make
sure they got the information and to see if
we could provide them with anything else.

8) After the promotion was over, we sent thank
you notes to everyone who participated,
including the media.

We covered everything a promotion is all about with
this event. We hit every media outlet available, and we
received excellent coverage from both newspapers in town,
all TV stations, and, of course, the live remote on one of
them.

We projected the image that matched the identity we
were trying to create. And, except for the fact that I was
interviewed on live television in a really goofy penguin suit,
our ideas and organization made for a quality promotion.

Not all promotions are like the one above, and not all
of them are as successful. Not all of them are as big or
involve as many people to make them work. And, there are
many factors to be aware of that can cause a promotion to
sour.

I once began working on the grand opening of a new
marina that was scheduled to open on a lake in Colorado.
It was going to be great! We were going to sponsor fishing
tournaments, boat rides, and raise money for a local char-

ity. The Governor was going to attend. It was going to be the best thing I had ever done!

A month before the event, a very windy storm hit the area and blew the marina into tiny bits of steel and sawdust. Things happen.

Not every promotion will work exactly as you have planned. Some work better than others. That's the nature of the beast. Multi-billion dollar corporations have staged promotions that fell flat on their faces. Remember "Herb" from Burger King? Flop. Coke changed its formula. Flush. Wall street tried to set records. Crash.

You design your own promotion by generating ideas and making them work. Use our Halloween promotion as a guide. Not every promotion has to contain all these elements, but every one should contain at least a few of them. You can make almost anything work if you try hard enough.

The fact that you're having promotions is enough. No matter what you do, you're making an honest attempt to stimulate interest in you and in your business. And that's public relations.

Now, let's design a promotion for you and your firm.

## ACME WIDGET CELEBRATES FIRST YEAR ANNIVERSARY

You remember Acme Widget, the manufacturer of widgets and consultant to the widget industry, from earlier in the book. In April they will celebrate their first anniversary in business. They've been following everything in the book up to this point, and now it's time for their big bash. With this promotion, they're going to cement their identity into the minds of their market and the community in general.

### The Brainstorming Session

Bob Jones, owner of Acme Widgets, gathered his employees after work one day for the brainstorming session. They sat around the conference table and talked ideas while his secretary took down all the ideas. Bob felt it was important to have his employees sharing this with him because as each of them had a particular knowledge of a particular function of Acme.

Bob kicked off the session by going over some of his ideas, telling the group what new products they could expect in the very near future. He got them thinking about possibly tying in with a new product with Acme's anniversary.

Then Bob got his staff rolling by sharing some of his thoughts on the promotion. He opened the floor for discussion. It started off a bit slowly, as do most of these sessions, but it soon picked up to where Bob's secretary had a difficult time keeping up with the flow of ideas. At the end of the session, they had come up with the following:

1) A First Anniversary wine and cheese party for present and potential widget customers, consulting clients, and the press, at which time they would introduce the new X-007 Wonder Widget. (Great for a media gathering, especially if you can provide some good food and cocktails.)

2) Acme could promote a First Anniversary sale featuring the new X-007 Wonder Widget.

3) They could tie into Easter by sponsoring an appearance by the Easter Bunny followed by an Easter Egg Hunt at the local

children's hospital. (Especially good for TV coverage.)

4) They might sponsor photos with the children and Easter Bunny at the local mall, the proceeds being donated to the children's hospital. (Great for a live remote any night of the week.)

With these ideas, they developed the following plan:

This particular year, Easter Sunday happens to fall on April 3rd.

## Date Schedule:

1) *Thursday night prior to Easter Sunday*:   Stage party for clients and the press beginning at five P.M. (This will allow people to stop on their way home from work.) Introduce the new X-007 Wonder Widget. Kick-off weeklong anniversary sale.

2) *One week prior to and through Saturday*:   Photos in the mall with the children and the Easter Bunny. (Proceeds will go to the Children's Hospital.) Possible live remote.

3) *Saturday morning, the day before Easter Sunday*: Easter Egg Hunt at the local children's hospital. Think TV coverage, newspaper photo-opportunity, and good news story.

## Press Release Schedule:

1) First Anniversary Announcement: Why is this important? How has Acme contributed to industry changes? Is anyone surprised that Acme is still in business after a full year? What effects have they had on the

community? Hand deliver first release two
weeks in advance.

2) The Acme group will draw attention to the
Children's hospital with the Easter Egg
Hunt. If the hospital has its own PR people
(which most hospitals do), Acme will work
with them throughout the promotion. They
may even get the hospital's PR department
to send out a few releases on their
letterhead with Acme's name as the sponsor.
Regardless of what the hospital does, Acme
will release the information on its own
letterhead one week prior to the event.
Notes to the TV stations inviting them to
the event will be enclosed. They will be told
who to contact once they arrive and where
they can set up.

3) Acme will send, or hand deliver when
possible, the announcement of the photos of
the Easter Bunny and the children in the
mall to benefit the Children's Hospital. It
will be delivered one week in advance of the
starting date. They will enclose notes to TV
stations inviting them to set up a live remote
any night of the week, making themselves
and a few members of the hospital staff
available for interviews. One of the TV
stations may choose to broadcast portions of
their programming from the mall close to
Acme's Ester Bunny.

4) The announcement of the X-007 Wonder
Widget with product, photos will be handed
to all media who attend Acme's VIP wine

and cheese party. Acme will hand-deliver the releases the next day to those media members not in attendance.

5) When the event is over, a recap release will be sent to the media on the success of the event. It will detail the amount of money raised for the hospital and will include a photo of Bob Jones handing a check over to the hospital administrator.

Depending on the logistics of your event, you may have to notify some official agencies, like the police, fire, sign code enforcement people, etc. Acme's celebration doesn't require notifying any official agency.

Invitations can be made inexpensively and in a very short time. I've found that the best are simple post cards with the invitation printed on the back. They cost less to print and less to mail. They get the point across and allow some room for creativity.

## The Aftermath

Follow-up phone calls should be made to all VIP's: the press and special accounts. (By now, Bob at Acme already has friends in the media who will be anxiously awaiting news from his company.)

Thank you notes should be sent to all involved, including staff, the hospital, the media, the mall, and whomever they find to dress up in the bunny suite and take the pictures.

The total cost of Acme's event will be minimal. Eggs, inexpensive wine, cheese and crackers, photo costs, and bunny suit rental. The whole promotion should cost under $300.

Now, assuming the event is over and done, what did all this get Acme, and why did they go through it all? For one thing, they got press coverage on all three local TV stations, both newspapers, and two radio stations, creating a great awareness of their company in a one week media blitz. It solidified their image as an active, concerned, caring, and positive business member of the community.

The promotion as a whole projected a good solid sense of Acme to their present clients and created an awareness with future clients. A good amount of money was raised for the hospital, and a few kids had a chance to laugh and smile for a morning.

The promotion was inexpensive and didn't take nearly as much time as it may sound. It's simply a matter of paying attention to your company, taking pride in what you are doing, and helping others at the same time. That's public relations, and public relations simply makes good business sense. Your company can do the same. Follow these guidelines and you'll be on your way to making your company a successful and viable entity in your town.

# CHAPTER 6

# ADVERTISING INTEGRATION
## Double Your Exposure

Advertising in a public relations book? Yes. As your business grows, so does your need for increased marketing efforts.

Advertising plays a huge part in the marketing plans of any size business. In fact, some advertising qualifies as public relations on its own. We're going to examine your advertising, how to buy it, and how to integrate it with your public relations program for a more effective overall marketing program. Integrating your PR efforts with your advertising will boost your exposure, help cement your identity in the minds of your market, and maintain positive and profitable relations with your customers.

All advertising supports, enhances, and reinforces all your marketing efforts. Your print advertising reinforces your radio advertising, which enhances your TV advertising, etc. All of this advertising should tie in with your public relations if you are to maintain the continued development

and solidification of your identity in business. *Theme* and
*Identity*: This is what people know and remember about
your business. It is how they perceive your business when
they think about it when they make a purchase, when they
make a recommendation, or when they just talk it over
lunch.

Some say that public relations is just another form of
advertising. Its the opposite. Advertising is a form of public
relations. Advertising is just more blatant and obvious call
to action. The more you promote your image, the greater
your image becomes and the more recognizable your business becomes. This is public relations.

Many good books have been written on advertising, so
I'm not about to write one here. I am going to talk generally
about media, showing you how each medium works in a
public relations sense. Also, I'm going to tell you how to
buy advertising effectively and inexpensively.

You don't tie in your advertising with your PR plan by
simply taking ads. You do it by developing the right kind
of ads, and placing them in the *most effective* media.

In a promotion, your advertising will almost always
automatically integrate with the theme of your promotion.
However, this is short term. In the long run, you should
develop your advertising strategies to include and revolve
around the common image and identity you have chosen
for your company.

## ADVERTISING IN GENERAL

Advertising takes many shapes and forms. From your basic
"Big Three" media (TV, radio and newspaper) to magazines, race cars and signs, to pens, post cards and license
plates, to matchboxes, coffee cups and flyers, to billboards,
buildings, and blimps, advertising inundates the average

American brain to an almost incomprehensible degree. And there's no sign that its going to let up one bit!

Hundreds of thousands of companies and organizations out there are trying to get your attention, and they're spending record amounts doing it. Why? Because it works. The competition is tough, and getting your message to your markets is even tougher.

Like your telephone, your copy machine, your computer and your car, advertising is a tool and should be thought of as such. It is your tool to get your market to do business with you. Before you get started, there are seven fairly basic questions you must answer:

1) What exactly are you advertising? A sale? Special product introduction? A change in the company?

2) To whom are you advertising? Who needs to get this message?

3) What is the best way to reach them? (The *Best*!)

4) What can you reasonably afford and how much should you spend on your advertising? (While you may have $5000 to spend advertising this event, do you have to spend it all?)

5) What message do you want to send your customers, and how do you want them to react? (What do you expect the consumer to do? Buy your product? Stop by and look? What are your exact expectations of your target markets, and how do you plan to get them to react the way you want them to? Otherwise known as a "call to action." "BUY

NOW!" "ORDER TODAY!" "STOP BY
OUR STORE TOMORROW!")

6) How will this advertising enhance your
promotion, and how will it fit your image
overall?

7) Finally, how can all the above be exploited
via the public relations techniques you have
learned up to this point?

These are the basics for any advertising you may do.

The key words in buying all your advertising are *Reach*
and *Frequency*. How many people in your target market see
your advertising, and how often do they see it? All advertising purchases are based on these two words. Each outlet
(radio or TV station) in each medium can tell you approx-
imately how many persons or households they reach. Some
of their figures are accurate, some of them are not. Sometimes you have to be careful.

You will rate all your advertising on a "Cost Per Thousand" (CPM) basis. In other words:

| Media | Cost | Households |
|-------|------|------------|
| Newspaper | $250 | 35,000 |
| Radio | $500 | 30,000 |
| TV | $750 | 45,000 |
| TOTAL | $1,500 | 110,000 |

$$CPM = \$13.63$$

Your CPM is $13.63. This means it costs you $13.63 to
reach a thousand people. Always keep track of your CPM.
You can use it to judge the efficiency of your advertising.
Say, for example, you run a radio promotion and you sell
150 widgets from that promotion with a CPM of $16.67.
Next you run a direct mail/newsletter promotion and sell

150 widgets with a CPM of $11. You know where to put your money to work more effectively. Not that you shouldn't make use of a good media mix. You don't want to miss anyone. But, when you know which medium is more cost effective, you will know where to put the bulk of your dollars. If you're selling much higher priced goods at a lower volume (Rolls Royces or Lear Jets) your CPM will undoubtedly be higher.

## DIRECT MAIL AND NEWSLETTERS

Direct Mail is probably one of the least expensive methods of advertising. If done properly, it can be very effective.

You can design a direct mail campaign for a specific event, a special sale, or an announcement; or you can develop a direct mail campaign as an ongoing entity of your company. You can use it as a staple in your advertising program.

The monthly newsletter with product and personal notes is effective and inexpensive because it lets your customers and potential customers into your company on a more personal level.

A newsletter need not be anything fancy. Tidbits of information about your company, short features on your employees, customer satisfaction letters, this month's special deals, etc., can all be included. Printing and typesetting are inexpensive. And if you have a computer, any good graphics program will help you put together a fine newsletter in no time.

If you just want to handle the basics (writing, naming what goes into the newsletter, etc.), small companies are springing up all over the country that will handle all your direct mail needs. Many printers are now involved in direct mail, and they can handle everything from your layout and design to your bulk mailing permit and actually getting the mailing to the post office. Many newspapers also have direct mail services.

## NEWSPAPERS & PRINT ADVERTISING

Newspaper advertising is probably the advertising with which business persons are most familiar. From the moment your business opens its doors and your phone is installed, your very first call may very well be from your local newspaper salesperson.

Newspaper advertising is purchased on a cost per column inch basis. *Always* sign a contract with your newspaper. Your advertising rates go down the more you advertise. Check with your individual newspaper, but in most cases the contract you sign will not necessarily lock you into having to spend a fortune on your print advertising. It will simply guarantee you the lower rate once you reach a certain point in your advertising. Newspapers are getting creative in their advertising contracts. In many cases, the lower contract rate can be rebated to you in the form of discounts over your subsequent purchases.

If you do not use all the advertising the contract specifies, you will simply be invoiced at the higher rate at the end of your contract. Or, you will be billed the make-up amount at the end of the contract term, which means you'll have longer to pay for it.

If you go over the amount of advertising specified in your contract, in most cases you will automatically receive the lower contract rate.

A good newspaper advertisement stands out from the crowd, has a distinct visual hook (a picture, drawing, or some other form of graphic), concisely tells the reader what he or she needs to know, and calls them to action. Probably the best way to stand out from the crowd is to use color in your newspaper advertising. One color may be more expensive, but the odds on the reader noticing it and retaining the information are vastly increased. (Be careful as to the color you choose. Some colors run by newspapers can be pretty atrocious.)

In many cases, you may request where you would like your ad placed in the newspaper. You may request a "right reading page." (When you open the newspaper, it's the page on the right). This is the best location for people to read your ad because it's the first one they see when they open the paper. In some cases the newspaper may do it at no charge, or you may pay a little extra. In most cases, they may just note your request and ignore it. If they can do it, they will. If not, they won't. But it's always good to at least make the request.

Most local magazines have relatively limited subscriptions. In fact, many local magazines are give-aways. Be very careful when you advertise in local magazines, because their circulation may not be all of what they tell you. They may *print* 50,000 copies, but they may have only 10,000 subscribers. The rest of their "circulation" relys on newsstand sales and give-away copies. On the other hand, a good magazine can offer what other print media generally can't — glossy color in your ad. Again, always request a right-reading page if at all possible.

## RADIO

Radio is one of my favorite media because it literally forces me to be creative. You can also target your message toward your market more than with most other media. Simply, certain types of people in certain age categories listen to certain types of stations that play their kinds of music. The most popular disc jockeys are paid small fortunes to attract and keep their audiences.

With radio, never pay the going rate. Your ad rep will

keep you abreast of all the current special packages which you might make use of. These packages will give you X number of spots during the course of each day. "AM and PM Drive Times" (when people go to and from work in the morning and evening) are the most expensive times, but all radio packages will include some of your spots in those time frames.

When you buy radio, your invoice will include the times when each of your spots ran. You should match these to the original designs of the package you purchased. Say you bought a package that offered two spots a day in drive time, two evening spots, and ROS ("Run of Schedule" — they put them where they want) a day. Your invoice should reflect that.

Nearly all radio stations offer live remote packages at fairly reasonable prices. Live remotes on good stations with good radio personalities are worth their weight. A live remote brigs the radio station to your door. While the records are still being played at the station, the radio personalities are in your business, talking to people, mentioning where they are each chance they get, etc. Live remotes include the following:

1) Three to five hour broadcast from your place of business

2) X number of your advertisements the week prior to the remote

3) X number of mentions and promotions during the DJs' chatter

4) All engineering and set up charges

Talent fees for the personalities are almost always extra, although you may be able to work something out with them.

Live remotes are fun. They're fun for you, they're fun

for the customers, they're fun for the radio personalities, and they're effective. So often people want to see what their favorite radio personalities really look like. After all, they only know them by their voice.

Creativity is the key to your radio advertising. As with all advertising, you should develop a theme so that listeners will hear the introduction to your ad and know from whom the ad is coming. The worst are dull radio ads. Let your brain go when thinking of a radio ad. Those that are a little off-center, a little odd, make for the best radio ads.

Use voices and sound effects to create exciting images for your listeners. If you don't think you're very creative, radio stations employ creative people to handle that department. Stress that you want you ad exceedingly creative, and they'll do it. If you don't like the results, have them do it again. You're the advertiser, and you have a right to expect results for your money.

## TELEVISION

As with radio, you buy on a cost-per-spot basis. Again, as with radio, you never want to pay the going rate, which is generally reserved for national advertisers and people who don't know any better. Most of the time your ad representative with the TV station will put together a package for you that works out to be significantly less than the going rate.

Every February, May, July and November, all the networks and local stations have what are known as "Sweeps Weeks." During these time periods the ratings services monitor each network and station to find out just who is watching what shows.

The results from these periods determine the advertising rates the stations will charge for the next few months.

Consequently, you'll notice that many of the **blockbuster TV events** occur during sweeps weeks.

Some stations give away prizes like boats and cars to entice you to watch their stations. Other stations have so far as to feature stories on the families involved in the ratings to boost the rating of their local news. Now that's bold! In any event, talk with your ad rep, and look for a package.

Television is expensive.

Why? Because it reaches so many people with pictures, words, and sounds. As a rule, you use television when you want to reach a large general audience. Yes, certain types of people watch certain types of shows, but the most you're going to get out of your ad rep is how many men and women between certain age groups watch what shows.

Your best bet is to buy ROS (run of schedule) or some sort of a package deal. You'll get a few spots on the midnight to six A.M. shift, but that's OK. TV stations generally aren't so terribly cruel or so stupid as to put all your spots on at that time.

In most cases, your package will include simple production (still shots, product photos, storefronts, etc.). If you want anything more elaborate, you have to spring for it on your own. And TV production is Expensive with a capital *E*.

Television stations divide their time blocks into the following:

The Dead Zone — midnight-six A.M.

Morning news & talk

Daytime

Early news

Early fringe (just before prime time)

Prime time

Late fringe (just after prime time)

Late news

Late night

These times change a bit depending on your time zone. Stick with ROD or a package, and you're bound to get a prime spot or two, and a few in the fringes. As with radio, keep your production simple and try to impart that **one** message that you want to get across.

You normally only have thirty seconds, so keep your message as simple and concise as possible. Service, price, product, reputation, where to go, and DO IT — period.

(*A word about live remotes*: Live remotes have become a staple in electronic journalism. Television stations spend hundreds of thousands of dollars on the latest nifty equipment such as monitor-filled trucks, etc., and they are compelled to use it all.

The theory is that the stations now have the capability to broadcast from anywhere "as news happens." Interestingly enough, not all car wrecks, earthquakes, stabbings, shootings or hostage-takings happen between 6:00 and 6:30 P.M. Besides, the remote trucks work a whole lot better when they know in advance what's going to happen.

Now that you're making news with your event, you can make use of a station's truck. If you're having a special event that seems appropriate for a live remote, suggest it to the stations that have them. In smaller markets, the odds are pretty good that you'll get one. In larger markets, it's a crapshoot.

Occasionally car wrecks, stabbings and shootings do happen between 6:00 and 6:30 P.M. So even though you're scheduled for a live remote, it may get sidetracked to something more dramatic.

Radio live remotes are almost always purchased. So unless the real Elvis is coming back to your store, don't count on any radio station volunteering its equipment.)

## CO-OP AND SPECIAL PROGRAMS

The cost of advertising has risen significantly over the past several decades, and naturally, product manufacturers want to get as much exposure for their advertising dollars as possible. Hence, the evolution of the coo-op program. Co-op funds equal free money. Say that ten times, and you'll realize just how important it is.

### FREE MONEY!

If you have any suppliers, manufacturers or wholesalers, investigate the possibility that they offer co-op programs. A co-op program, simply defined: If you sell a certain manufacturer's product, that manufacturer gives you money to market it in the form of co-op advertising funds.

Those companies that do sponsor co-op programs generally do so on a matching basis. For example, if you spend $200 on an ad featuring a manufacturer's product, that manufacturer will give you $100 toward that ad up to a certain percentage of your gross sales of that product.

Say you sold $10,000 of Acme Widgets last year. This year, they may co-op up to five percent or more of those sales as long as you use the money to advertise your company and Acme Widgets. If you are a retail store with a number of suppliers and manufacturers, your options are limitless.

Many manufacturers will also sponsor co--op funds for your appearances in trade shows, mall exhibitions, special events and other promotions. So it's not just advertising that they'll spring for, it could be a whole array of marketing tools, techniques and ideas!

Through the effective use of co-op funds, you can expand your advertising budget two- or sometimes three-fold over what your own budget allows by following a few simple guidelines. These guidelines are spelled out for you by the manufacturer in whatever guidebook they provide, and they're really very simple. Many co-op programs offer ad "shells," featuring their product with space for your company's name. Just insert your name, and you're off. No muss, no fuss.

If you have a manufacturer that doesn't offer co-op funds, try asking him. Cut a deal! The root of our economy is cutting deals, so why not try? Say to your supplier, "I'll pick up half this ad with your product if you pick up the other half." The worst that can happen is that they'll say no, and you'll ask someone else. All you're doing now is setting up your own co-op program.

The sad part is that around sixty percent of all coo-op funds go unused throughout the course of the year. This is **free** money in exchange for a little paperwork. So be a little aggressive.

## THE TRADEOUT

The tradeout is a common practice in the advertising field. The tradeout is the simple exchange of goods and services for airtime or advertising space. You don't think the general manager of a radio station drives a BMW for nothing? If he does, you can probably assume it's in exchange for advertising on his station.

Tradeouts are good in some instances, but remember the golden rule of tradeouts — *You Can't Eat Trades*. Trades put zero money in your pocket, and more often than not the media get the better end of the deal.

On the other hand, tradeouts can be beneficial in certain circumstances. Weigh exactly what you're trading for what your getting in return, and make sure it's fair to you.

## A LOOK AT HOW PEOPLE ADVERTISE

*Cars/Trucks:*   Theoretically, everyone is in the market for a car, so the prevailing advertising for them is designed to **GET YOUR ATTENTION!** Because so many cars exit from so many manufacturers, the efforts to create an identity for each car or each line are staggering. Consequently, your television rocks with **BLUCKBUSTING** prices, **INCREDIBLE** deals and **UNBEATABLE** interest rates. Full page ads appear in your newspaper, and your ears twinge when Larry Loudmouth of Larry's Auto Barn screams at you over the radio. Nevertheless, the ads get their points across.

*Kitchen Products:*   They dice, slice, walk the dog, start your car, wax your floor, and are guaranteed not to bag, sag, lag, drag, or make you old before your time. Ronco made these ads famous on late night TV. There's a method for it, though. It's called *Product Demonstration*. Showing the product in use is one of the best ways to sell it.

*Beer:*   It is said that we elect presidents the same way we buy beer: We don't buy beer, we buy the image of a beer. In short, all products have images created around them.

As consumers, we buy those products that best represent the image we like for ourselves. This is the basis of much of the advertising we see today from beer to politicians.

*Furniture:* Those store selling expensive furniture target their advertising in the media that are most likely to be seen or heard by people of a certain age, income range, and taste: non-rock/easy-listening radio stations, glossy/lifestyle-type magazines, etc. Lower cost furniture stores appear on TV, in the newspaper, and on the radio: more rock stations, more drawings in the paper, greater emphasis on things like cost, financing, etc.

*The Package:* A smart way to sell...a smart way to buy. Everything is sold in packages these days. A boat comes fully equipped with a trailer and accessories for one price. A trip includes airfare, hotels, rental car, etc., for one price. Cars are now generally equipped with everything from the manufacturer. Banks offer packages in the form of an account with free checking, credit card, an easy access credit line, ATM card, overdraft coverage, and varying interest rates for varying deposits. Furniture stores offer home and condo packages at special prices. Can your item be packaged in any way to enhance it's value in the consumer's mind? If so, it will undoubedly make it more salable.

# CHAPTER 7

# EMERGENCIES AND BEYOND
## Graduating To An Agency

You must always be prepared for any emergencies. Few of us ever plan for them to happen; they just do. And while PR may not seem like an important consideration at the time, even somewhat macabre to think about, be able to prepare yourself quickly.

Emergencies can be anything: a severe fire at your place of business, a major accident adversely affecting one or more people, a defective product that injures someone, or even rumors that surface accusing you or someone in your company of something that may or may not have occurred.

You can generally count on little or no advance warning. Most likely, you'll be very busy thinking about anything but the press at this particular time. But, the public perception of the whole affair will ultimately depend on your handling of the crisis.

The most important thing to remember in an emergency situation is to convey a sincere sense of *openness, honesty,* and *responsibility.* While you can't be sure of everything that goes on in your business, ultimately everything that happens there is your responsibility. You're the final word on everything, especially in a crisis situation.

Most reporters will understand your preoccupation with an emergency situation. They may walk with you, shouting questions, but that's their job. The scene is tense, and they're doing the same thing you are — looking for answers.

The best way to keep reporters happy and away from you while your making important decisions is to set up a press area. Even if just one reporter is following your story, he or she will appreciate a place near the action, near a phone, with some fresh coffee and a donut or two. Generally, follow the procedures you used for a successful press conference.

## WHAT TO SAY & WHEN TO SAY IT

1) Be honest, and never say anything until you're absolutely sure it's true and correct.

2) Never speculate on causes, but act as quickly as possible to find the causes and explanations. If you don't know, just say "I can't be sure of that yet," or "I don't know. We're still trying to find out."

3) Never overreact or cause others to overreact.

4) Never use humor in any circumstance. It always tends to get misconstrued. Everything about the situation is serious, and you should act accordingly.

5) Offer as much help to the press as possible in terms of specific information. Accuracy is

key. If a diagram or photo works best, use
them.

In general, make it as easy and comfortable as possible
for the press. Never hide anything, because it may come
back to haunt you. Even if it's embarrassing, you're just
going to have to fess up.

## GRADUATION — TO USE AN AGENCY?

If you practice the principles in this book, your business
should soon be thriving. You may be doing your own PR
so well you may not have time to handle it on your own.
Since you know you can't do without a public relations
program, you may now wish to hire a person or agency to
handle the job for you.

At this stage of the game, there are many options. Do
you need a full-service ad/PR agency? Can you get away
with using a local free-lance writer? How much can you
afford? How grand a program do you wish to maintain?

You can answer all these questions by examining the
size and performance of your company. Its needs and your
goals will dictate the size and scope of your program.

It's key to remember that you're hiring talent. The
performance of that talent is almost impossible to accu-
rately calculate in advance. (There are various figures that
have been used in calculating the effectiveness of your PR
dollar spent. For example, for every dollar you spend in
PR, some say you should receive $2 to $4 dollars in coverage or more *Some* say this. I say do whatever works and gets
your customers in the door.)

When hiring an agency, the only real judge you will
probably have is what they have done for other clients...and
how much they charged them. Unless you're about ready
to dump a million dollar account in their laps, you can't
really expect them to develop an entire program for you

on spec. However, it is not unreasonable for you to ask for
a fairly detailed summary of what they plan to do your
you...and how much it will cost. (Get this in writing.)

Most advertising agencies offer PR services. Since the
two go hand-in-hand in some respects, and the talents
meld and crossover in many areas, it makes sense. Monitor
your agency carefully. Meet *all* the players in advance, from
the guy writing your releases to the top gun of the company. Get ready for a lot of handshakes and smiles as they
aim for your account. Make sure it doesn't stop after you
sign up. I've seen it happen time and time again: You sign
up with an agency, and after meeting the president, the
creative director, the account supervisor, the account executive, the secretary, and the janitor, you never hear from
a soul other than your account executive. It's so important
that you're there and involved in every move your PR
agency makes on your behalf. After all, they are your PR
"representatives."

A good PR agency is creative, punctual, aware, connected, affordable, and attentative to you and your needs.
A good PR agency also listens to you. After all, you know
your company better than anyone else. When you tell them
what you want done on your behalf, they should listen and
complement your ideas with their own.

You should have to "sign-off" on every press release
and photo that goes out of their office.

## A WORD ABOUT FREE-LANCERS

Every city has legions of free-lance writers, photographers,
and artists. Can you rely on them? Usually. If you're calling
the shots in your PR program, a good free lance writer can
take the place of hiring an agency. You'll save a lot of
money, too.

He or she will walk in with a portfolio of articles, and

you'll know in an instant how they rate. Remember, writers, photographers and artists can be a curious breed, so don't be alarmed if they're a bit off center at first. In fact, I tend to be suspicious of a writer you always see in a three piece suit and well-tended-to hair. Talent takes many forms, and you're hiring substance not looks.

Free-lance artist should possess an intimate knowledge of both the creative and mechanical processes required to take an image from the mind to the printed page. You will know if you simply ask how it's done. It all should roll off their tongues. They too will have portfolios of prior work. Pick one whose work fits the image you want for your company. A good logo from a local agency will run anywhere from $250 to $2,500 depending on whom you hire.

All free-lance fees will be lower than agency fees because you're not employing the agency's secretarial help, janitorial services, etc. Free-lancers can do a very good job. Just remember, you're in charge of all they do. It will be less work than doing everything on your own, but you'll still be actively involved by being in charge of strategy and planning.

Many college students are available for this type of free-lance work. Many of them are quite good, and they're always eager to build their portfolios before graduating from college.

Look at what you can afford, think about free-lancers, and decide for yourself which direction you're going to take.

# CHAPTER 8

# MAKE IT HAPPEN!
## That's Public Relations

Only you can make PR work for your company. It's simple, really: If you follow just a portion of what this book has tried to convey, you'll be farther ahead than most other people in your business.

Public relations is our link to those people you want to affect. If done honestly, it is effective. I can't stress how important honesty is in any PR program. In this day and age, with so many of the "professionals" clouding the airwaves and newspapers with confusing, insensitive, and vicious political promotion, countless promotions of useless or sometimes harmful products, and inane hype for the sake of hype on nothing in particular while spending a ton of the client's money. Simple, honest promotional marketing can be highly effective.

In spite of what is made of the press by politicians, media watchdog groups, and others, I hope you realize that the majority of the people in the press aren't mad,

95

vindictive ogres waiting for the chance to jump on unsuspecting victims. They're like you and me, and they have their jobs to do. And they need you for news.

The press release is not some magical sorcery created by brain trusts in Washington, New York or Chicago. It is written by people like you and me to be read by people like you and me.

Press conferences are not just for politicians and CEO's. If you have something important to say, you can say it just as effectively as any senator or representative. Who's to say your news isn't just as important? To some people it's probably more important.

Public relations is your tool for the proper beneficial exposure for your company. This exposure means profits.

### Remember Acme Widgets?
### It Can Happen To You

The person in charge of Acme Widgets bought this book in August. He then drafted a plan like the one in the very first chapter of this book. A staff meeting/brainstorming session started the whole company thinking news. They all began coming up with story ideas to promote their own company. Then they introduced themselves to the press. They put together media lists and began sending information to the media on the industry, their company, and their products. They began requesting information from their suppliers, etc.

In November, the new X-35 widget came onto the market. Acme introduced this amazing little gem to the community at a press conference at their offices. The fanfare was so great that people were breaking down the doors to buy them.

By December, Acme's owner had indeed become the local industry spokesperson. This not only meant that his contacts at the media were recognizing him when he called, it meant that he was actually getting calls from the press on anything that had to do with widgets. Each time Acme got a call, they were in the newspaper. They will continue this program into the future, and they will grow into a success-ful company with a good, quality image in the minds of their customers, their potential customers, and the public in general.

It doesn't take long to set the wheels of a good PR program in motion. And, as you've seen, the main tools are you're mind and a few pieces of paper.

Don't be shy. The worst that can happen is that you may have to try a little harder at what you're doing. Public relations is all a part of that.

Someday, somewhere, a potential client or a possible sale may just kick himself in the back of the head and say, "Oh yea, I've heard of them! They're good."

**That's public relations.**

# ADDENDUM

We are very interested in your successes for future editions of *Power PR*. So please let us know how the book has helped you with your own PR program, press release, promotion, etc. Please address your replies to:

*Power PR*
Fell Publishers, Inc.
2131 Hollywood Blvd.
Hollywood, FL 33020

# APPENDIX
## Sample
## Press Releases
## and
## Newsletters

10/15/89

NEWS FROM HARBOR POINT

FOR IMMEDIATE RELEASE

**HARBOR POINT.**
Address
Phone

### PETER PENGUIN PROMOTES HALLOWEEN SAFETY

Peter Penguin, Harbor Point's Halloween safety mascot, is waddling to area Elementary schools, Pre-schools and Day-care centers in northeastern Colorado Springs presenting Halloween safety tips to young trick or treaters.

Peter and his brother Edward Penguin will help host Harbor Point's safe Halloween on Thursday, October 31st from five to seven PM at the Harbor Point model home centers. Children and their parents are invited to attend this traditional Halloween, during which all of Harbor Point's model home centers will be open for Trick or Treating.

Peter and Edward are hoping to see many of their new friends Halloween night.

--30--

For Further Information:

Dennis C. Hill

Marketing Director

Harbor Point Corporation

(419-555-1930)

10/25/86

NEWS FROM:

"THE DENVER BOAT SHOW '87"

# THE DENVER
# BOAT SHOW '87"

**Address**

**Phone**

### "DENVER BOAT SHOW" SLATED FOR
### JANUARY 22nd-25th @ CURRIGAN HALL

The Denver Boat Show, Colorado's largest boat show, is slated for January 22nd-25th at Currigan Hall, 14th and Champa Sts., in downtown Denver, according to Don Lewis, President of the Colorado Marine Dealers Association.

"I'm pleased to note that this year's show will be the biggest boat show ever in Colorado," Lewis said.

The entire 100,000 sq. ft. of Currigan Hall's main floor was filled immediately with dealers from Colorado and neighboring states, according to Lewis. Some remaining space is available on the lower level.

Last year's event drew more than 10,000 boating enthusiasts. This year's show will feature the latest motorboats and sailboats on display, special financing rates, and a variety of events and seminars.

For more information on the remaining exhibition space, please contact show organizer Jim Janty, Exhibitor Showcase, Ltd., (303) 590-7717.

--30--

For Further Information:

Jim Janty

6547 N. Academy Blvd., #510

Colorado Springs, Co 80909

(303) 555-1234

3/6/88

NEWS FROM MILLPOZ, INC.

FOR IMMEDIATE RELEASE

# MILLPOZ, INC.
**Address**

**Phone**

### NEW LCM MINE READIES PRODUCTION FACILITIES

MILLPOZ, INC., a Colorado mining venture, is putting the finishing touches on its Southern Colorado plant and mine. They are expected to begin full operations by April 15th, 1986.

The company will be mining POZZOLANA (trade name - POZ PLUS), a lost circulation material for the oil drilling industry that is expected to dominate the market in the very near future.

"It is the most effective material for drilling needs, and drillers will enjoy working with it," according to John Smith, Vice President in charge of mine operations. "It's light, available in manageable bags, and the drillers will find themselves filling voids more efficiently and cost effectively."

Drilling company management will enjoy POZ PLUS for its cost effectiveness — a ton costs about half of the nearest comparable material. And, since POZ PLUS is lighter, the company will get more quality material per ton, affecting even greater cost savings.

--MORE--

# MILLPOZ, INC.

**Page 2**

    For further information, contact HILL*TOP Company, exclusive marketing agent for POZ PLUS to the oil drilling industry at (213) 555-1234.

--30--

For Further Information:

Dennis C. Hill

Hill*Top Company

1234 E. Fisher St.

Los Angeles, CA 12345

(213) 555-1234

6/31/87            **ABC Construction**

NEWS FROM ABC CONSTRUCTION      **Address**

FOR IMMEDIATE RELEASE          **Phone**

### SHOWCASE OF HOMES '86 BEGINS IN WOODLAND PARK

Four Woodland Park homebuilders have joined together to present "Showcase of Homes '86" to the public in Woodland Park, according to Donald Jones, Vice President of ABC Construction Co., Inc., one of the participants.

ABC Construction, Homes Plus Corporation, Smith Builders, Inc., and O'Brien and New Concepts, Inc., all of Woodland Park, are all participating in the Showcase, which will run on weekends through July 6th.

"This showcase represents an alternative to driving to various locations to view the types of homes that each offers," said Jones. "We're all growing with the community of Woodland Park, and the showcase gives us each a chance to establish ourselves as quality-minded area builders."

All four homes are located in the Woods Estates subdivision on the North side of Highway 24 in south Woodland Park, according to Jones. They range in price from $97,900 to $149,900.

"Showcase of Homes '86" is free of charge and open to the public on weekends from 11 am to 6 PM, and it will run through Sunday, July 6th. Refreshments will be available.

--30--

For Further Information:

Donald Jones, V.P.

ABC Construction, Inc.

123 Highway 24

Woodland Park, Maine 02678

(408) 555-1234

11/25/85
NEWS FROM IAFP
FOR IMMEDIATE RELEASE

# International Association of Financial Planners

Address
Phone

### RICHARDS TO ADDRESS IAFP

John Richards of Atlanta, GA, will be the featured speaker at the Thursday, Dec. 5th meeting of the Cleveland International Association of Financial Planners (IAFP). Mr. Richards' presentation will concentrate on the changes in federal reserve policies and their impact on investments over the next ten years.

Mr. Richards is President and CEO of Richards, Inc., an Atlanta-based firm specializing in tangible asset investments. He is also Chairman and founder of Richards and Associates Consulting, Inc., a firm monitoring all hard asset markets. In addition, he serves on the Board of Directors of Jack Jones Enterprises, a financial consortium headed by leading financial analyst, Jack Jones. He was recently appointed to the Marketing Council for Materials Management (MCMM), a national lobbying group based in Washington, D.C.

The Dec. 5th presentation will be held at the Holdiay Inn Downtown, 3rd Ave. and 14th St. The cost is $5. For further information and reservations, please call Mr. Joe Sanchez, IAFP Program Director, at Sanchez Financial Services, Inc., 555-1234.

--30--

For Further Information:

Mr. Joe Sanchez

Sanchez Financial Services, Inc.

(407) 555-1234

6/11/89

NEWS FROM SMITH PHOTOGRAPHY

FOR IMMEDIATE RELEASE

**SMITH PHOTOGRAPHY**
Address
Phone

### JOHN C. SMITH AWARDS ZOO POSTER

Kay C. Jones, local resident and CPA with ABC & Company, won the original John C. Smith poster, "Snow Birds," in a drawing held at Saturday's "Wildlife Art Festival" at the Bronx Zoo.

The poster, designed to raise money for the zoo's on-going expenses, is on sale in the zoo's gift shop. The poster may also be purchased directly from John C. Smith's studios. All proceeds from the sale of the poster benefit the zoo.

--30--

For Further Information:

John C. Smith

615 5th Avenue

New York, NY 12345

(212) 555-1234

4/29/89

NEWS FROM PEOPLE IN REAL ESTATE

FOR IMMEDIATE RELEASE

**PEOPLE IN REAL ESTATE**

Address

Phone

### TABER NAMED VICE PRESIDENT OF HILL CONTRACTING

Donald R. Taber has been named Vice President/Director of Operations of Hill Construction Co., Inc., announced Peter Retton, President. Taber was formerly Project Manager for the Miami-based company.

A 13-year veteran of the construction business, Taber has been with Hill Construction for the past four years.

A Louisiana native, Taber relocated to the Miami area in 1980, and has recently completed his Florida Real Estate License.

Hill Construction is a Miami construction firm serving Dade and Broward Counties.

--30--

For Further Information:

Donald R. Taber

Hill Construction Co., Inc.

274 W. 49th Ave.

Miami, Florida 12345

(212) 555-1234

2/24/88

NEWS FROM RUMORS

FOR IMMEDIATE RELEASE

# RUMORS
**Address**

**Phone**

### RONNIE MORRIS TO APPEAR AT RUMORS

By special arrangement, popular recording artist Ronnie Morris will appear at Rumors (251 W. Main St., Catskill) this Saturday night, February 27, beginning at 9 P.M.

Morris plays a variety of pop tunes and original songs. He has performed extensively on the East Coast and has performed with such acts as Pure Prarie League, Greg Allman, Tom Chapin, The Outlaws, Elvin Bishop and The Grass Roots.

As always, there is no admission charge at Rumors. For further information, please call Rumors at 555-5050 after 5 P.M.

--30--

For Further Information:

Dennis C. Hill

231 W. Main Street

Catskill, NY 12414

(518)555-1234

3725 Austin Bluffs Parkway, Colorado Springs, Colorado 80918        May 9, 1989

To my old time readers, I need to apologize. This is my first news-letter in about one year - I am sorry that I procrastinated about it.

MOTHER'S DAY - MAY 14  We will open at 1 PM and we are featuring three entrees. They are:

Roast Loin of Pork

Stuffed Filet of Sole ———————— $7.75

Breast of Chicken a la creme

all are served as full dinners with salads, vegetables du jour and appropriate potatoe or rice. We will serve right through until 11:30 PM. Reservations are strongly suggested.

ONE NEW AND EXCITING DEVELOPMENT AT McKENNA'S - We are now doing a full blown DINNER THEATRE on Fridays and Saturdays (we started in March). The show is a musical review - an olio of Broadway - Fats Waller - 50's and 60's nostalgia. It is being performed by a lively and talented cast of ten who really are having fun doing what they are doing. We seat for dinner at 6:30 PM and the show starts at 8:00. We offer a choice of 3 entrees each night and your wait staff are your cast of performers. The show lasts until 10 pm and is appropriate for all ages. The cost for the dinner and show is $15.75. Dessert and adult beverages are extra. Start-ing in June - we will be going 5 nights each week through the summer (Tuesday - Saturday) with two new shows and casts with the show alternating every week.        Reservations are necessary.

SUNDAY NIGHT - FOLK NIGHT  For 2½ years, Frank Moore and Phil Volan have been the mainstays in our Sunday night program. They have been joined most weeks with some sort of guest performer(s). Two weeks ago, Phil left us - so we have had to a look at this program. Frank will be playing on Sundays along with guest artists through the end of June (except May 21 when we have booked a large banquet). We now start our Sunday night program about 6:30 pm and go until about 9:30 pm. Then July and August will be vacation time for the folk music. The folk music will be back in September with a new and exciting program.

FREQUENT DINER MENU  For those of you who have not been in for a while, we have added to the menu a series of 11 items for dinner that are in the more affordable category. They include things like: meatloaf, chicken fried steak, spaghetti, liver and onions . . . . They are all priced under $7.00 and are designed to be something that you can have if you dine out several nights a week but are on a tight budget. So come on by and try them.

Hope to see you all soon.

Jim

Healthy HEART NEWS

Vol. 1, No. 1
Winter 1989

This newsletter is published quarterly for your information by doctors Greenberg, Blonder, and Tulin. 635-7172

This issue:

Cardiac Technology In the 90's

Good News for Chocoholics

# February Is Heart Month

Celebrating Valentine's Day this month is an ideal reminder to do something for your heart that you may not have done in the past year. These things include:
- **Blood Pressure Checked by Professional**
- **Blood Cholesterol Checked by Professional**
- **Exercising Once to Three Times A Week**
- **Initiate A Low Fat/Low Cholesterol Diet**
- **Quit Smoking**

Resources available to assist you in these areas include:
- Our professional staff which can offer guidance in these areas. Please call 635-7172.
- **American Heart Association** has available helpful literature and dietary classes available at 601 N. Nevada. #635-7688.
- **American Cancer Society** - "Fresh Start", Smoking Cessation Group Program. 555 E. Pikes Peak Ave., Suite 105, #636-5101.

## Cardiac Technology Heads Into the 1990's

*Dr. David Greenberg*
Technology in cardiology is evolving at a very active pace as we are heading into the 90's. The focus of this expansion in technical capabilities is in regard to therapeutic cardiology. The use of lasers are one of the hottest topics in technical capabilities that falls into this category.

There are currently five lasers that are being evaluated on an experimental basis, for the treatment of coronary artery disease. The possibility does exist that one of these lasers may be available here in Colorado Springs to assist in the evaluation of a laser treatment therapy for improving coronary blood flow in patients. This will likely be used in conjunction with current balloon angioplasty.

There are almost 20 current devices being evaluated across the country as treatment modalities to improve coronary blood flow from a non-surgical standpoint. One of the devices that may be used is called atherectomy. This device is used to shave and remove fatty plaque from the coronary artery and then removed by a catheter. PREVENTION OF ATHEROSCLEROSIS IS OUR FIRST LINE OF DEFENSE. Not only are we excited about these new technologies on the horizon, but we will continue to encourage all our patients to learn the importance of prevention and risk factor modification in Coronary Artery Disease.

## Patient Education Meetings

We continue to have our patient education classes on the third Wednesday night of each month. These classes are open to all patients, spouses or family members who wish to learn more about the prevention of heart disease. We will meet at the Health Association Building on 12 North Meade from 7:00 to 8:30 p.m. and would appreciate a call if you plan to attend any of the meetings. There is no charge for these classes.

**March 15th:** *Cardiac Technology In the 1990's*, presented by Dr. David Greenberg.

### Insurance Information Corner

Introduction to **Health Maintenance Organizations** (HMO) have raised some complicated issues over the past two years. Familiarizing yourself with the HMO payment guidelines prevents you, our patient, from being primarily responsible for payment of your bill at the time of services.

The most important guidelines to follow, streamlining the payment process, includes:
- **Verify that the cardiologist,** your Primary Care Physician (PCP) is referring you to, **participates in your HMO plan.**
- **Bring a referral form** from your PCP at the time of your office visit or procedure. Without this form, you become responsible for the payment of services.
- **Know your HMO Plan.** We are here to answer any questions you may have at 520-1131.

**IRMH** Indian River Memorial Hospital

# Physicians' Update

A Monthly Publication
for our
Medical Staff
from the President

November 1989     Vol. 1   No. 7

## Strategic Planning

On Nov. 13, Paul Keckley, president of the Keckley Group, will be leading an all-day seminar on "Strategic Healthcare Planning for the Nineties" in the third-floor classroom of the Human Services Building. Although we recognize it is difficult for you to set aside a day in your schedule, particularly a Monday, we have invited any of you who are able to attend to do so, and to confirm your intentions by calling ext. 1101.

Mr. Keckley has been invited specifically to speak to our boards and several key committees as a prelude to the development of a detailed strategic plan for the hospital. He may be involved in further aspects of that planning, and as physicians, you certainly will be involved, which is why I hope you will have a chance to hear him. Beyond that, his ability to localize national healthcare trends and issues is outstanding, and I believe you will find it is a day well spent.

If you are not able to attend, but would like to take part in our strategic planning process, please let me know. In the years ahead, we can not completely avoid difficult issues. I would like to believe that we can face them with respect for each other and, most of all, for the patient, and furthermore, that conflict on one issue does not preclude cooperation on another.

## E.R. Gets New Physician Group

A new, private group of emergency physicians that will serve only IRMH joined the staff in October. The small group is expected to bring stability to the emergency department. Two members, doctors Brad Damiani and Richard Peters are IRMH emergency room veterans. Only one member, Dr. John Nerness, practices outside the hospital.

Dr. Luis Rivera heads the group, along with associates James Dozier, M.D. and Michael Mattice, M.D. Doctors Rivera and Dozier first met when they were emergency medicine residents in New York city in 1984. Four years later, they found themselves practicing together in the emergency room of HCA Lawnwood Regional Medical Center in Fort Pierce.

The pair presented their idea for a small, private group serving only IRMH and then recruited other physicians who shared their philosophy.

Medical Director Luis Rivera is a New York native who studied medicine at Rutgers Medical School in New Jersey before going on to an internship and residency in New York City. He's practiced emergency medicine for six years and expects to sit for certification by the American Board of Emergency Medicine this month.

Like Dr. Rivera, Dr. Dozier completed his residency at Long Island Jewish-Hillside Medical Center in New York City. The Kentucky native has five years of emergency medicine experience and is certified in emergency medicine.

Dr. Michael Mattice studied medicine at Michigan State University in his home state, before moving to Oregon for his internship and residency. He's certified by the American Board of Family Practice and sat for certification by the American Board of Emergency Medicine late in October.

Dr. Tomas Jacome is a native of Panama who's certified by both the American Board of Emergency Medicine and the American Board of Pediatrics. He studied medicine in Bogota, Colombia and had an internship and residency in Kentucky.

Dr. John Nerness is a board-certified OB/GYN who sat for his certification in emergency medicine late in October. Dr. Nerness was born in Malaysia, where his parents were American

can missionaries. He went to Loma Linda University's College of Medicine in California and stayed there for his internship and residency.

## Self-Insurance

Because carefully planned self-insurance can be a sound business move, the hospital has decided to self-insure its underlying coverage. So, too, has a group of physicians approached us to suggest a change in the hospital policy which currently requires outside insurance coverage, in order that they might insure themselves. The hospital Board of Directors, after careful consideration of the proposed trust agreement, asked the hospital attorney to respond with his comments by Oct. 1, and the physicians' counsel to respond to those by Oct. 31. It is the board's intention to review the trust agreement at its November meeting to determine whether it presents an acceptable alternative to the hospital's existing policy of requiring professional liability insurance coverage.

## Office Staff Luncheon

Your office staff — receptionist, office manager and/or nurse — is invited to an information-sharing luncheon at noon, Thursday, Nov. 16 in the third-floor classroom of the Human Services Building. Mike Garrett, Director of The Surgery Center, Barbara Gervasio, Surgical Services Nursing Director, and Brad Pearse, Director of Imaging Sciences, will be there to speak and address concerns. For those who are able to stay, the luncheon will be followed by a one-hour class on AIDS, as this is a topic which your office staffs have asked that we provide more information on. We hope you will encourage attendance among your office personnel, as this is an excellent means for improv-

(continued)

# NOR'WOOD NEWS

Number 8

## NOR'WOOD DEEDS 77-ACRE COMMUNITY PARK TO CITY

*Soccer And Softball Complexes Start*

The deed to a 77-acre community park in Nor'Wood was officially transferred to the City of Colorado Springs Thursday, July 25th, according to Kent Petre, President of Nor'Wood.

Preliminary construction on the grounds was started by Nor'Wood, and the first phase, which will contain soccer and softball complexes, will be completed by mid-September. They will be playable in the spring of 1986.

"We're very excited about this project," Petre said. "We've been working with the Parks and Recreation Department for a long time, and all the park staff were instrumental in making this park a reality. We will soon be able to provide quality soccer facilities for the community, which are long overdue."

Following the completion of Phase One, construction will be geared to future amenities that will include tennis courts, racquetball courts, picnic area, a community swimming pool, walking and jogging trails, and a community center.

Much of the park will remain in its natural state, according to Petre.

Designed by Jim Reece and Fred Mas of the Park staff, the park will be linked with a comprehensive open space system that flows through Nor'Wood's 2,400 acres. The park is boundried on the North by Cottonwood Creek, Dublin to the

Kent Petre, President of Norwood, hands deed to Cottonwood Creek Park to City Council woman, Mary Ellen McNally.

South, and Rangewood Drive to the East.

Nor'Wood Development Corporation is a local development concern specializing in the areas of commercial, industrial and residential real estate.

## NICKLES HOMES MOVES TO NOR'WOOD

Nickles Homes, Nor'Wood's newest homebuilder, has announced plans for the construction of a series of homes on 25 lots in Nor'Wood. The

continued on page 3

# EISENHOWER MEDICAL CENTER

# PROGRESS

**VOL. 2 NO. 1**            **SPRING 1986**

## EMERGENCY DEPARTMENT NEARS COMPLETION

Emergency Room gets new look with covered drive-through entry.

Dr. Gregory Tietz lays the last brick.

Sunny spring skies in Colorado (for the most part) continue to aid construction crews in timely completion of Eisenhower's building expansion.

Employees and patients alike try to exhibit patience throughout the noise, vibrations, odors and inconvenience as the completion date draws nearer.

Enthusiasm is easy to summon these days, however, as the new Emergency Room entrance (pictured above) begins to look like the genuine state-of-the-art facility it will soon be.

Late May is the time targeted for ER construction to end. During June "the move" will take place, and hopefully by July operations and procedures will be running smoothly enough for an Open House.

The Medical Office Building is expected to be completed in August.

The IRMH

**channel**

Published for Our Employees and Friends    **Vol. 1  No. 11    November 1989**

## "Children Can Help" is Theme for Emergency Medicine Week

The Indian River County Commission adopted a resolution proclaiming Sept. 17-23 as Emergency Medicine Week in Indian River County. The theme for the celebration was "Children Can Help."

To learn how they can help, third graders in all county schools were invited to submit posters with a safety message. More than 500 students entered. Winners were announced for each school and then the judges selected a county-wide grand prize winner.

This year's winner was Kenny Aderne of Pelican Island Elementary School, for his poster on the danger of flying kites near power lines.

Kenny appeared on the television program "Vero Beach Live" with chief paramedic Jim Judge and IRMH emergency department nurse **Rosanna Crawford**, R.N. On Sept. 22, Kenny was taken to school in an ambulance with the sirens blaring and his name announced over the ambulance's loudspeaker. His third-grade classmates greeted him with cheers and escorted him into school.

IRMH Emergency Services Director **Helen Baker**, R.N., praised all those who helped teach the students safety.

"The program helps focus attention on safety habits and is beneficial in giving

children helpful information on what they can do in an emergency," she said.

Kenny's prize-winning poster is on display in the emergency department.

*Emergency room nurse **Alan Fitz**, R.N., teaches school children about safety during Emergency Medicine Week.*

*Third grader Kenny Aderne of Pelican Island Elementary School got the message of kite safety across with his grand prize-winning poster in the county-wide contest.*

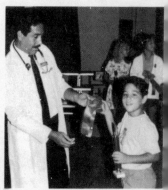

*Emergency physician **Lou Rivera**, M.D., gives artist Kenny Aderne a ribbon and trophy during a special ceremony at Pelican Island Elementary School.*

# On Center

### TORRANCE MEMORIAL MEDICAL CENTER

Vol. 1, No. 1                                                        July 1993

## Torrance Memorial Unveils Preview of Progress

### TORRANCE MEMORIAL MEDICAL CENTER

The name Torrance Memorial has come to represent much more than just an acute care hospital. That's why, beginning July 1, the facility became known as *Torrance Memorial Medical Center*.

"We need to recognize that we're rapidly developing into a full-service medical campus," stated Mark Costa, vice president/Administration, in reference to Torrance Memorial's development and expansion of a wide range of state-of-the-art medical services. "While our acute care hospital services continue to be our major focus, we are broadening the scope of who we are, and our name needs to reflect this."

"Changing our name to 'Torrance

Memorial Medical Center' helps clarify our identity as a major medical center with several missions, including acute hospital services, ambulatory services, health education, and, in the future, long-term care," added Sally Eberhard, vice president/Planning and Marketing.

In addition to the name change, Torrance Memorial's logo has been updated for the first time in 11 years, she said. "We have nothing to lose, and everything to gain in terms of how Torrance Memorial is perceived in the community," stated Eberhard of the subtle changes. Eberhard and Costa, members of the medical center's Strategic Planning Committee, worked closely with the Board of Trustees in updating Torrance Memorial's corporate image. "We realize we have developed quite an established, readily identifiable look over the years.

(continued on page 4)

## Meet On Center

Torrance Memorial's monthly employee newsletter has a new name and look. *On Center*, as the publication is now called, is designed to represent our expanding focus as a community medical center. Reflecting both the facility's new name and updated logo, the larger, more flexible format will allow for more in-depth news coverage, an increased number of feature articles, improved use of photographs, as well as easier reading.

As always, *On Center* is intended to keep Torrance Memorial employees informed about events and issues that affect them and the medical center, as a whole. In addition, it provides a forum to recognize employee accomplishments and to showcase departmental activities. It is hoped that the new format attracts greater reader interest and involvement in the newsletter.

## Resources Management Gets Results!  • • • • • • • •

The log book has gone the way of the dinosaur in Torrance Memorial's Emergency Department.

It's all part of an effort to save time for both patients and the Admitting staff through computerization of the emergency admissions process, according to Beth Ames, Admitting supervisor.

Each year, the Emergency Department treats an average of 24,000 patients. In the past, this has translated into about 4,000 hours on the part of the Admitting staff, who were required to manually log each patient's name, address, age, sex, admitting/discharge time, Emergency Department physician, private physician, discharge diagnosis, services rendered and more, according to Ames.

Through computerization of the nearly three-inch thick Emergency Department log book, Ames said, "We're much better able to stay on top of things during peak admitting hours in the Emergency Room, and now we can even obtain a complete listing of a day's Emergency Room visits by nine o'clock the next morning!"

"I think it's fantastic. It saves a tremendous amount of time," added Mike Hosino, Admitting representative, of the June 1 changeover to computerized logging. "Not only does it speed up the Admitting process, but it also frees up more of our time to devote to other aspects of our job." An additional benefit is an estimated savings of $7 per patient on medical malpractice insurance, due to the perceived high accuracy rate of the newly automated tracking process, Ames said.

Finding better ways to approach a job which result in improved productivity, quality of services, or in reduced costs is the concept behind Torrance Memorial's Resources Management program. Begun in early spring, this 12-week program provides team members, such as Ames, with the tools they need to take a fresh, new look at their jobs.

"Resources Management changed my

*Mike Hosino tries out the new computerized emergency admissions process developed by Beth Ames (right).*

way of thinking. I look at things now and wonder how we could do them better." Ames added that she hopes to have the Emergency Department's census on computer within the next month.

"The process is so creative you don't think anything is impossible anymore," added Debbie Banderas, R.N., supervisor, Post Partum. Banderas' Resources Management project was to replace her department's current breast cream, used by new mothers to ease the breastfeeding process, with a product containing Lanolin. "The cream we were using contained alcohol and other unnatural ingredients which needed to be wiped off before each feeding. By going to the Lanolin product, there is no need to wipe off the cream before breastfeeding, because it is a pure product (made from natual ingredients). This makes it much more convenient to the patient," Banderas said. Additionally, the Lanolin product is preferred by most physicians and

community groups, including La Leche League, she said.

Banderas will also be saving the department an estimated $5,846 annually, a decrease in cost of $2.90 per tube of cream.

Although this has been a change Banderas wanted to make for quite a while, she said she was put off by what she felt would be a lot of red tape. "My first instinct was that in order to get the physician order sheet changed, a physician would need to initiate the project. But I found our OB's (obstetricians) to be very supportive of the idea."

"It's amazing how many resources we have available to us in this hospital," stated Banderas. "It was really rewarding for me to be able to contribute to the hospital's profitability, while making a change that would enhance the quality of patient care. Resources Management doesn't just stop here. I plan on doing future projects, now that I have the tools."

1

# Reflections

Vol. 2, No. 2      Indian River Memorial Hospital, Vero Beach, Florida      Fall, 1989

## Congratulations to Aftercare Grads

New Beginnings congratulates the following individuals who recently graduated from a year of aftercare: William M., Fred S., Sam J., Billy P. and Alda K.

Our aftercare therapist, Betty Moore, says, "each of these individuals has worked very hard throughout the year and contributed to the weekly group."

Best wishes to all of you. Keep coming back. It works!

## "Our Dream Comes True"
**Jan Archbold**, M.S., treatment coordinator

My dream since coming to New Beginnings two and a half years ago has been to do inpatient co-dependency treatment. That dream came true on Oct. 9, when we admitted five patients to our new three-week intensive inpatient co-dependency program.

Our co-dependency program has been designed with the same dedication and commitment to quality care that we have in treating chemical dependency. The treatment team and our corporate professional services department have researched and developed the program. Careful attention was

given throughout to insure that our chemical dependency program would be enhanced by the addition of a co-dependency program and that co-dependents would be best served by exposure and some shared group experience with the chemically dependent patients. The end result is a very comprehensive quality program for both chem deps and co-deps.

We hope all of you are as excited as we are about our new co-dependency program and thank you for your continuing support.

For more information about our co-dependency or chemical dependency programs, please call us at 562-9206. And again, many thanks to all of you who helped make a dream come true.

## In Memorium

On Tuesday, Aug. 8, our staff lost a very dear friend and colleague when staff psychologist Alvin Wooten, Ph.D., passed away.

Dr. Wooten was well known for his many contributions, including the professional journal articles he wrote and forensic services he provided to the public defenders office.

Before he began working with the New Beginnings staff in 1986, Dr. Wooten had careers as a military psychologist and an adjunct professor at several universities. At New Beginnings he provided clinical feedback to the therapy staff on all our patients. He guided the therapy team members in their clinical and therapeutic decisions for each patient.

We've all benefitted from Dr. Wooten's involvement with New Beginnings and have been enriched by his knowledge and keen perception of the disease of addiction.

## New Faces at New Beginnings

**Helen Murray-Shaw** joined our staff in August as a family therapist. Ms. Shaw relocated with her family, from the Orlando area, where she worked as a co-dependency counselor and DUI instructor. She's completing her course work for a master's degree in counseling at Rollins College.

**Ralph Mora**, Ph.D., became our consulting staff psychologist in June. Dr. Mora is a familiar face to many of us because he served as the clinical director of Rivendell Hospital from 1987 to 1988. Dr. Mora earned his doctorate degree in psychology at Adelphi University in 1983. He has a private practice working with individuals suffering from addiction and related illnesses.

**Sherry Ellis**, S.A.T., recently joined the nursing staff as a substance abuse tech. Ms. Ellis worked as a tech at Fort Pierce Detox prior to working with New Beginnings. She is enrolled at Indian River Community College earning her certification in substance abuse treatment.